Contents

The *Steck-Vaughn Reading Workout* series includes four books that have been carefully leveled to ensure readability and increase the likelihood of success. The series is designed to reach middle-school students who need practice with reading strategies and other literacy skills. The passages are high-interest/low readability to promote interest. The reading levels for each book are as follows:

Book	Grade Level
1	2.5–3.0
2	3.0–3.5
3	3.5–4.5
4	4.5–5.5

Steck-Vaughn Reading Workout is organized into two units with two fiction and two nonfiction selections per theme. Each selection is supported by the following activity pages.

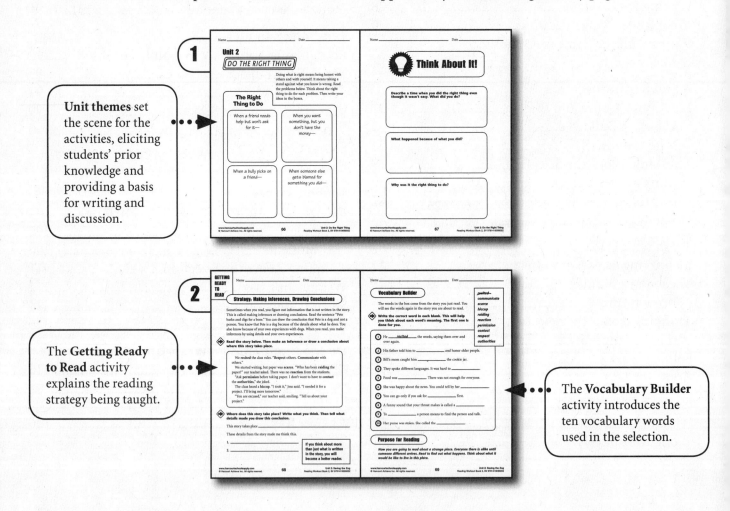

Unit themes set the scene for the activities, eliciting students' prior knowledge and providing a basis for writing and discussion.

The **Getting Ready to Read** activity explains the reading strategy being taught.

The **Vocabulary Builder** activity introduces the ten vocabulary words used in the selection.

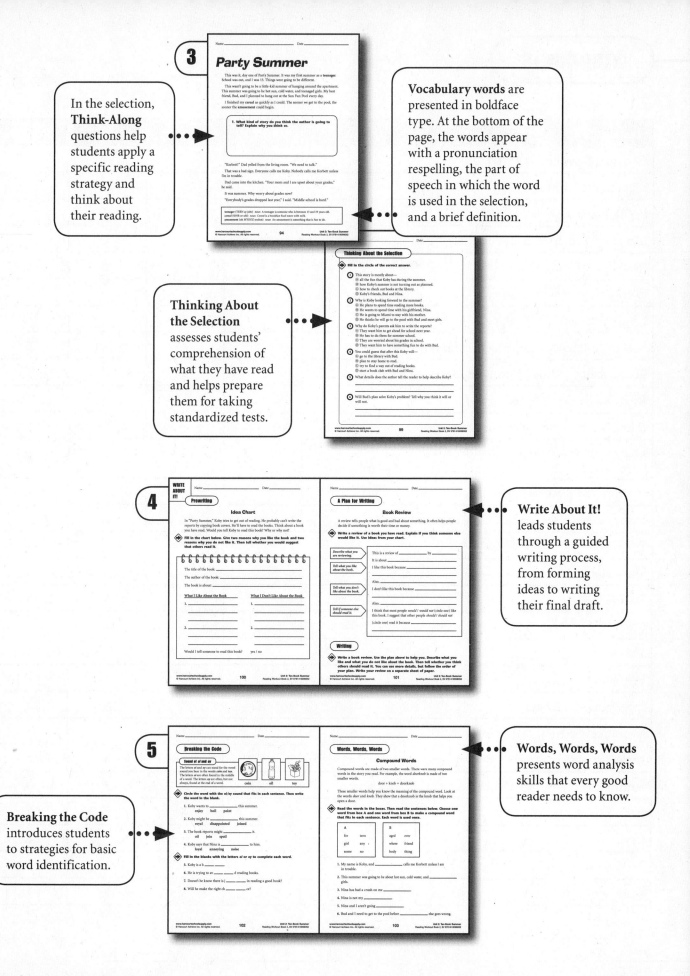

In the selection, **Think-Along** questions help students apply a specific reading strategy and think about their reading.

Vocabulary words are presented in boldface type. At the bottom of the page, the words appear with a pronunciation respelling, the part of speech in which the word is used in the selection, and a brief definition.

Thinking About the Selection assesses students' comprehension of what they have read and helps prepare them for taking standardized tests.

Write About It! leads students through a guided writing process, from forming ideas to writing their final draft.

Words, Words, Words presents word analysis skills that every good reader needs to know.

Breaking the Code introduces students to strategies for basic word identification.

Standards

Strategy/Skill	Book 1	Book 2	Book 3	Book 4
GENERAL READING STRATEGIES				
Making predictions	X		X	
Recognizing sequence	X		X	
Identifying main idea and details	X		X	
Identifying facts and opinions	X		X	
Comparing and contrasting		X		X
Identifying cause and effect		X		X
Making inferences/drawing conclusions		X		X
Recognizing author's viewpoint and purpose		X		X
READING STRATEGIES: NONFICTION				
Using headers and subheaders to guide reading			X	X
Using informational text features (including table of contents, index, and glossary)			X	X
Interpreting pictures, graphs, and charts			X	X
Using research skills and strategies to extend a topic			X	X
READING STRATEGIES: FICTION				
Story plot			X	X
Setting			X	X
Character			X	X
Theme			X	X
WRITING FORMS				
Informational Essays	X	X	X	X
Narratives (stories, real or imagined)	X	X	X	X
Letters	X	X	X	X
Summaries	X	X	X	X
Instructions	X	X	X	X
Reviews	X	X	X	X
Persuasive Essays	X	X	X	X
Speeches	X	X	X	X

Strategy/Skill	Book 1	Book 2	Book 3	Book 4
WORD IDENTIFICATION STRATEGIES: PHONICS				
Short and long *a*	X			
Short and long *e*	X			
Short and long *i*	X			
Short and long *o*	X			
Short and long *u*	X			
Variant consonants – *g*	X			
Variant consonants – *c*	X			
Variant consonants – *s*	X			
Initial, medial, and final consonant digraphs – *ph, gh*		X		
R-controlled vowels – *er, ir, ur*		X		
R-controlled vowels – *ar, or*		X		
Vowel digraph – *oo*		X		
Sounds of *ow*		X		
Sounds of *ou*		X		
Diphthongs – *oi, oy*		X		
Silent consonants – *kn, wr, gh*		X		
WORD ANALYSIS				
Using context clues	X	X	X	X
Understanding compound words	X	X	X	X
Interpreting multiple-meaning words	X	X	X	X
Identifying synonyms and antonyms	X	X	X	X
Understanding/using homonyms, homographs, and homophones	X	X	X	X
Using prefixes, suffixes, and roots of words	X	X	X	X
Interpreting figurative language (including similes and metaphors)	X	X	X	X
Using reference materials (including dictionary and thesaurus)	X	X	X	X

www.harcourtschoolsupply.com
Standards
Reading Workout Book 2, SV 9781419099052

Unit 1

COUNT ON ME

Being responsible means that people can count on you to do what you should. Think about responsibilities people your age have. Write them in the boxes below.

Responsibilities

To our families:
doing chores at home

To our friends:

To our teachers:

To ourselves:
doing our best at everything we try

Name _____ Date _____

 # Think About It!

Think about a time when you were responsible.
What did you do?

How did others count on you?

How did you feel afterward?

Unit 1: Count On Me
Reading Workout Book 2, SV 9781419099052

Name _____ Date _____

Strategy: Comparing and Contrasting

Finding out how things are the same and how they are different is called *comparing* and *contrasting*. You compare things when you think about how they are alike. You contrast things when you think about how they are different. Comparing and contrasting can help you understand new information. Also it can help you think · in a new way about what you already know.

 Read the passage below. Think about what happened. Is it different from what the wrestler thought would happen?

> The **wrestler** thought he was ready for the match. He felt **rugged** enough for the **challenge**. People called him "Ever Ready."
>
> The match began, but his **temperature** was high. Without any **warning** signs, the wrestler passed out. Someone called the hospital.
>
> A **paramedic** raced up the **escalator** with a long **stride**. He got to the ring. The wrestler was lying down.
>
> "I feel OK now, but I'll **admit** I wasn't ready this time," the wrestler said. "I should be **renamed** 'Sometimes Ready.'"

 Was the match different from how the wrestler thought it would be? In the first box, write what the wrestler thought would happen. In the second box, write what did happen.

What the Wrestler Thought Would Happen	What Did Happen

The wrestler thought he was ready. He was not ready. Your answers in the boxes *contrasted* what the wrestler thought would happen with what did happen.

> **Comparing and contrasting will help you think about what you read.**

Vocabulary Builder

The words in the box come from the short passage you just read. You will see these words again in the story you are about to read.

 Write the correct word in each sentence. This will help you think about the words before you begin reading. The first one has been done for you.

~~temperature~~
challenge
rugged
renamed
warning
paramedic
escalator
stride
admit
wrestler

① The measure of heat or cold is called ___temperature___ .

② A _____ wins by keeping the other player on the mat.

③ A _____ is a long walking step.

④ If I _____ that I did something wrong, will I still be punished?

⑤ An _____ is a moving stairway.

⑥ The _____ raced to the fire to help anyone who was hurt.

⑦ The _____ sign said that the old building was dangerous.

⑧ If something was given a new name, it was _____ .

⑨ Running the long race was a _____, but I finished.

⑩ Someone who is strong and tough could be called _____ .

Purpose for Reading

Now you are going to read about two boys who skip school to have an adventure. They think they are too cool for school. Read to find out what happens.

Too Cool for School

Manny Brito rode his bike fast. Too fast. He headed straight for John Lomatiwa.

Every school morning, John waited on his bike in front of his house. Manny rode to meet him. When Manny saw John, he raced right at him. At the last second, Manny always hit the brakes.

"This time he'll crash into me for sure," John thought. He tried not to look worried.

Manny slammed on his brakes. He stopped just a few feet from John.

"Hey, John," Manny said, acting as if nothing had happened. "It's a cool day, right?"

"Right," John agreed.

Arizona is known for hot days. Summer is really hot. The **temperature** hits 110 degrees most days. It's too hot to do much outdoors.

Even in October, the temperature is often over 90. But today was different. It was 70 degrees and a nice day to be outdoors. It was also a school day.

"Too cool for school?" Manny asked.

> **1. What does a "cool day" mean to you? Write what you think.**

Manny was daring John to skip school. John didn't really want to skip. He liked school more than Manny did. But it was a great day to be free. "Sure!" he said. "Too cool for school."

"Cool enough for hiking Little Peak Trail?" Manny asked.

Another dare. John knew about the trail. It led up about a mile to the top of Little Peak Mountain.

The boys saw the mountain in the distance every day, but they had never hiked the trail. Other people said it was like climbing a mile-high stairway. It would be a **challenge** even on a cool day.

---

temperature (TEHM puhr uh chuhr) *noun* Temperature is the measure of heat in the air.
challenge (CHAL uhnj) *noun* A challenge is a task that is hard to do.

"No problem," John said. "I'm a **rugged** Hopi, remember?"

"I thought you were an American Indian," Manny said.

"Same thing," John answered. "I'm quick enough to beat you to the top."

"No way! I'll go up so fast, the trail will be **renamed** the Manny Brito Trail."

So the boys hit the trail, not the books. First they bought water. Then they rode to Little Peak. After an hour of tough biking, they arrived at the trail.

"See that post with the red phone? Let's lock our bikes there," Manny said.

"That's an emergency phone," John said. "It would be hard for someone to use the phone with bikes in the way." John worried about things like that.

"Like someone who sees kids skipping school?" Manny asked.

"Maybe," John laughed. "How about we just use that?" He pointed to a bike rack.

"My plan exactly," Manny said.

---

2. How is John different from Manny?

As the boys locked their bikes, they saw a **warning** sign.

DANGER!
Steep trail
People with heart or breathing problems should <u>not</u> climb.

---

rugged (RUHG ihd) *adjective* A person who is rugged is strong.
renamed (ree NAYMD) *verb* When something is renamed, it is given a different name.
warning (WAWR nihng) *adjective* Warning means "telling of danger."

"You'd better not hike," Manny said, pointing to the sign.

John smiled. "My only problem will be laughing too hard when a **paramedic** has to help you down."

Manny chuckled. "We'll see who's laughing in an hour."

At first the trail was easy. The boys started hiking quickly.

"This is nothing," Manny said.

John agreed. "It's like riding an **escalator**."

But the truth was a bit different. Both boys soon had sore legs and were soaked in sweat. Their walk slowed.

After twenty minutes, the boys spotted a stone bench.

"Want to sit?" asked Manny, who was breathing hard. He wasn't as tall as John. He had trouble keeping up with John's long **stride**.

"No way. I'm as fresh as the *piki* bread my mother made this morning," John answered between deep breaths. *Piki* is a special Hopi bread.

"Me, too," Manny gasped. "I just want to enjoy the view."

"OK," John said quickly. "It's worth a look." Neither boy would **admit** he was tired.

---

3. **Would you admit that you were tired? Explain how you would act like John and Manny or how you would act differently.**

---

paramedic (par uh MEHD ihk) *noun* A paramedic is a person who is trained to help people who are hurt.

escalator (EHS kuh layt uhr) *noun* An escalator is a moving stairway.

stride (STRYD) *noun* A stride is a long step in walking.

admit (ad MIHT) *verb* To admit something is to tell the truth.

The boys plopped down on the bench and drank some water. They caught their breath. The trail was almost empty. Then a strong-looking man ran past and nodded hello.

After the man was gone, John asked, "Did you see the muscles on that guy? He's built like a **wrestler**."

Manny said, "Maybe he's in the WWE."

"The Little Peak Monster?" John joked.

The boys laughed. They were ready to hike again.

> **4. Will the man have an easier or harder time climbing the mountain than John and Manny? Tell why you think that.**

---

wrestler (REHS luhr) *noun* A wrestler is a fighter who uses his or her hands to force someone to the ground without punching that person.

Name _____ Date _____

Thinking About the Selection

 Fill in the circle of the correct answer.

1. What is special about the weather on the day in this story?
   Ⓐ It is rainy.   Ⓒ It is hot.
   Ⓑ It is sunny.   Ⓓ It is cool.

2. Why doesn't John want to skip school?
   Ⓐ It is too hot outside.   Ⓒ Their class is taking a trip.
   Ⓑ John does not like Manny.   Ⓓ John likes school.

3. Why do the boys call the man the "Little Peak Monster"?
   Ⓐ The man sounds like a monster.
   Ⓑ The man looks strong.
   Ⓒ The man looks ugly.
   Ⓓ The boys are scared.

4. How is what the boys say different from how they feel when climbing?
   Ⓐ They say they are not tired, but they feel tired.
   Ⓑ They say they are tired, but they really want to look at the view.
   Ⓒ They say they like the mountain, but they wish they were in school.
   Ⓓ They say they are not hungry, but they want food.

5. Compare Manny and John. Describe one way in which they are alike.

   _____

   _____

6. Contrast Manny and John. Describe one way in which they are different.

   _____

Reading Workout Book 2, SV 9781419099052

Name _____ Date _____

Prewriting

Idea Web

In "Too Cool for School," Manny wants an adventure. John wants to be responsible and go to school, but Manny gets John to go with him. Make up a story about two friends. One friend wants excitement and gets the other friend to go along. Think of what might happen.

 Fill in the web below. Tell what the friends did. Tell how they were not being responsible.

Who these friends were and what they were like:

What the friends did:

How the friends were not being responsible:

Filling out this page will help you organize your ideas before you start writing.

Name _____ Date _____

A Plan for Writing

Out for Fun

A story tells about something that happened. A story can be real or imagined. Every story has characters who "act out" the story.

 Write a story about two friends. They want some excitement but aren't being responsible. Use ideas from your web.

Tell about the friends.	One day two friends, _____ and _____, were _____. _____ said to _____ that they should _____. At first, _____ thought they shouldn't because _____ _____.
Tell what they did.	They set out on the adventure anyway. Here's what they did. _____ _____.
Tell how they weren't being responsible.	They were having fun, but they were not responsible. Here's how. _____ _____.

Writing

 Write a story. Use the plan above to help you. Tell about two friends on an adventure. Tell how they weren't being responsible. You can add more details to make the story better. Write your story on a separate sheet of paper.

Name _____ Date _____

Breaking the Code

f sound of *gh* and *ph*

The letters *gh* and *ph* can stand for the sound of the letter *f* that you hear in the word *fan*. This is the sound you hear in *cough*, *alphabet*, and *dolphin*.

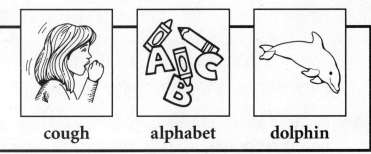

cough   alphabet   dolphin

 Circle the word with the *f* sound of *gh* or *ph* that fits best in each sentence. Then write the word in the blank.

1. John told Manny not to lock his bike near the red _____.
   phone   trophy   light

2. The hike was hard because the trail was _____.
   high   straight   rough

3. The man who passed them on the trail looked like a _____ man.
   fighting   tough   ghostly

4. John said he would _____ when paramedics carried Manny down the hill.
   laugh   sigh   photograph

 Circle the words with the *f* sound of *gh* or *ph* in the sentences below.

5. It was a pretty day in Phoenix.

6. The boys had enough water to take on the hike.

7. Manny thought the man looked as big as an elephant.

8. While the boys caught their breath, they saw a view worth a photograph.

Words, Words, Words

Figurative Language

Writers use figurative language to describe things in an unusual way and to help the reader get a better picture of what is happening in the story. A simile is one type of figurative language. Writers use similes to describe things by comparing them to other things. Similes begin with the words *like* or *as*.

In the story, John tells Manny that climbing the peak is "like riding an escalator," although climbing is not that easy.

Why do you think John compared climbing the peak to riding an escalator?

_____

 Read the sentences from the story. Tell what is being compared. Then explain how the simile helps describe what is happening in the story.

1. Other people said it was like climbing a mile-high stairway.

   Climbing the peak is being compared to _____.

   How does this help describe what climbing the peak is like? _____

   _____

2. "I'm as fresh as the *piki* bread my mother made this morning," John answered between deep breaths.

   John is comparing himself to _____.

   How does this help describe how John feels? _____.

3. He's built like a wrestler.

   The hiker is being compared to _____.

   How does this help describe the hiker? _____

Name _____ Date _____

Strategy: Comparing and Contrasting

Authors tell how things are alike by comparing them. Authors tell how things are different by contrasting them. When you read, words such as *like, same,* or *also* are clues that things are alike. Words such as *but* or *different* are clues that things are not alike.

 Read the passage below. Think about what is alike and what is different.

> Mountain climbers today are unlike climbers in the past. Climbers on an **expedition** today wear different clothes to keep them warm. Staying warm is important when the temperature is below **zero**. Climbers used to eat canned **sardines**. Today, food choices for climbers have **increased**.
>
> Climbers today are like climbers of the past. Climbers today **risk** their lives like climbers did in past years. They have the same need for **oxygen** when they are in a **zone** that is at a high **altitude**. Climbers today still want the **triumph** of reaching the **summit**.

 This passage shows how climbers can be alike in some ways and different in others. How are climbers today like climbers in the past? How are they different? Write your answers in the boxes below. Use clue words such as *unlike, like,* and *same* to help you compare and contrast.

How Are Climbers Today <u>Like</u> Climbers in the Past?	How Are Climbers Today <u>Different</u> from Climbers in the Past?

Comparing and contrasting will help you think about what you read.

Vocabulary Builder

The words in the box come from the passage you just read. You will see these words again in the passage you are about to read.

 Complete the puzzle below. This will help you remember each word and its meaning. The first word has been done for you.

altitude
risk
expedition
summit
sardines
zone
oxygen
zero
increased
triumph

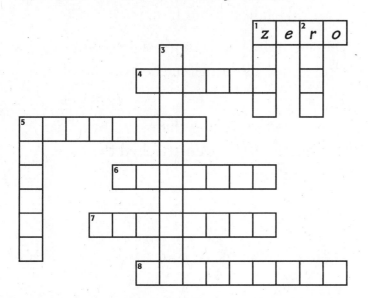

Across

1. This point lies one degree below one on a temperature scale.
4. We need this invisible gas to live.
5. These are a kind of small fish.
6. A big success might be called a _____.
7. This tells how high above sea level something is.
8. When something got bigger, it did this.

Down

1. This is an area or section.
2. If you take a chance, you _____ losing something.
3. This is a trip taken for a special reason.
5. If you reach the highest point, you have reached this.

Purpose for Reading

Now you are going to read about why people climb mountains. Mountain climbing can be dangerous, but climbers like the challenge. Read to learn more about these brave climbers.

Why People Climb Mountains

It was May 1953. Two men were climbing a dangerous cliff. They were thousands of feet high, halfway up the world's tallest mountain.

The mountain was Everest. It is 29,035 feet tall. That's an **altitude** of almost $5\frac{1}{2}$ miles. It is almost as high as 20 Empire State Buildings stacked on top of each other.

The two men were alone. If they fell, no one would hear their screams. Their lives depended on a rope that tied them together. The men attached the rope to hooks they pounded into the frozen mountain.

altitude (AL tuh tood) *noun* Altitude tells how high something is above sea level.

Suddenly the bigger man, Edmund Hillary, stepped on a loose chunk of ice. It broke. He fell off the mountain. The smaller man, Tenzing Norgay, braced himself.

The rope tugged him hard, but he was strong. With Hillary hanging below, Norgay took a deep breath. He pulled Hillary back up.

Why would two men **risk** their lives like this? Hillary and Norgay wanted to be the first to climb to the top of Mount Everest. No one had ever done it.

---

1. Tell about something you did that was very difficult. Compare it to what Hillary and Norgay were doing.

Did You Know?

Legend says that a large creature with four toes and red hair lives on Mount Everest. It is half man, half beast. People in the area, the Sherpas, call it "Yeti." English-speaking people call it "The Abominable Snowman."

---

risk (RIHSK) *verb* To risk something is to take a chance of losing that thing.

Two Brave Men

Hillary and Norgay began their **expedition** 3 months earlier. It started with almost 400 people helping them. These other people helped carry supplies. They also set up camps along the 175 miles of trails that led up Mount Everest.

Hillary was a shy man from New Zealand who longed for adventure. He loved to climb mountains.

Norgay was a Sherpa who grew up near Mount Everest. Sherpas are mountain people from the country of Nepal. Norgay loved to climb, too. He worked as a guide in the Himalayas, the mountain range where Mount Everest is.

In the 40 or so years before Hillary and Norgay's trip, climbers from ten other expeditions had already tried to reach the **summit** of Mount Everest. They had failed. Nineteen men had died, and two had disappeared.

Norgay and Hillary were determined to reach the peak. In fact, Norgay said that he would reach the top "or die."

2. How do you think Norgay and Hillary will be different from the climbers who failed?

By May 28, 1953, Norgay and Hillary had left their helpers behind. The two spent the night alone in a frozen tent 27,900 feet above sea level. It was the highest place that anyone had ever camped.

---

expedition (ehks puh DIHSH uhn) *noun* An expedition is a trip taken for a special reason.
summit (SUHM iht) *noun* The summit is the highest point of a mountain.

The next morning, at 4:00 A.M., they ate a breakfast of **sardines** and melted snow with lemon and sugar. Then they began the final stretch of the climb.

Both men wore 8 layers of clothes and carried 40 pounds of equipment. They moved carefully. They were in the Death Zone.

This **zone** is a dangerous area that starts at 25,000 feet. The air is "thin" there—it does not have much **oxygen**. Hillary and Norgay had to use oxygen masks in order to breathe.

The air is also very cold. It can be 100 degrees below **zero** on Mount Everest. The wind was so fierce that it could knock the men off their feet.

3. Why do you think this area is called the Death Zone?

Hillary and Norgay struggled up the mountain. Suddenly Norgay couldn't breathe. At first neither man knew why. Then Hillary saw that ice had blocked Norgay's oxygen line. Hillary quickly fixed the blocked line.

---

sardines (sahr DEENZ) *noun* Sardines are a kind of small fish.
zone (ZOHN) *noun* A zone is an area that is set off from other areas.
oxygen (AHK sih juhn) *noun* Oxygen is an invisible gas in the air that people need to breathe.
zero (ZIHR oh) *noun* Zero is the point that lies one degree below one on a temperature scale.

Soon the men saw the mountain's peak. To reach it, they would have to climb a thin ledge. To one side of the ledge, there was a drop of 8,000 feet. To the other side, the drop **increased** to 10,000 feet. If either man fell, he would die.

Taking one step at a time, they made it to the top. Hillary and Norgay had reached the highest place on Earth! They hugged each other to celebrate their **triumph**. Norgay thanked the mountain by leaving some chocolate in the snow. Hillary left a small cross.

What did they see on top of the world? "Nothing above us, a world below," Edmund Hillary said.

Why Climb Mountains?

Many people like Hillary and Norgay have risked their lives to climb mountains. Why do they do this?

Some people climb mountains to explore. They want to learn more about nature or themselves. Many like the challenge of doing something dangerous.

When asked why people climb mountains, a famous mountain climber named George Mallory had an answer. He said that people will climb a mountain "because it is there."

> **4. Why do you think some people like the challenge of doing something dangerous?**

---

increased (ihn KREESD) *verb* Increased means "became greater."
triumph (TRY uhmf) *noun* A triumph is a win or a success.

Thinking About the Selection

 Fill in the circle of the correct answer.

1. Which of the following is <u>not</u> true about the height of Mount Everest?
   Ⓐ It is the world's tallest mountain.
   Ⓑ It is 29,035 miles high.
   Ⓒ It is almost $5\frac{1}{2}$ miles high.
   Ⓓ It is almost as tall as 20 Empire State Buildings.

2. This passage is mostly about—
   Ⓐ what it is like to climb Mount Everest.
   Ⓑ what you need to climb mountains.
   Ⓒ different mountain ranges in the world.
   Ⓓ how to climb mountains.

3. Why did Hillary and Norgay want to climb Mount Everest?
   Ⓐ They needed to get to the other side.
   Ⓑ They were looking for lost climbers.
   Ⓒ They wanted to set up a camp at the top.
   Ⓓ They wanted to be the first to reach the top.

4. What makes the Death Zone so dangerous?
   Ⓐ The air is so thin that breathing is difficult.
   Ⓑ The mountain gets much steeper in this area.
   Ⓒ The clouds make it difficult to see.
   Ⓓ Oxygen tanks freeze at this height.

5. Compare Hillary and Norgay. What is one way they are alike?

   _____

   _____

6. Contrast Hillary and Norgay. What is one way they are different?

   _____

   _____

Prewriting

Idea Chart

In "Why People Climb Mountains," Edmund Hillary and Tenzing Norgay risked their lives to climb Mount Everest. They had to count on each other to stay safe. Think of something that you need someone's help to do. How would you tell someone how to help you?

 Fill in the chart below. Tell what the three main steps are and write details about how to do each step.

Something I Can Do: _____

Why I Need Someone's Help to Do This: _____

_____

Here Is How to Do It:

STEP 1	STEP 2	STEP 3
What I Do	What I Do	What I Do
What You Do	What You Do	What You Do

Filling out this page will help you organize your ideas before you start writing.

Reading Workout Book 2, SV 9781419099052

A Plan for Writing

I'll Show You How

Instructions tell how to do something. Instructions must be clear and in the correct order so that someone can learn from them.

 Write instructions to tell someone how you would work together to do something. Use ideas from your chart.

What you can do	I know how to _____. I need to do this with someone because _____ _____.
Step 1 with details	Here is how we do this. First I _____ _____. While I do this, you _____ _____.
Step 2 with details	Next I _____. While I do this, you _____ _____.
Step 3 with details	Finally I _____ _____. When I do this, you _____ _____.

Writing

 Write instructions to tell someone how to help you do something. Use the plan above to help you. Tell what you will do. Tell what the other person will do. You can give more details to help someone learn, but go in the same order as your plan. Write your instructions on a separate sheet of paper.

Name _____ Date _____

Breaking the Code

R-controlled vowels *er*, *ir*, and *ur*

When the letter *r* follows a vowel, it can change the sound that vowel makes. Say the word *pet*. Now say the word *pert*. Say the word *bun*. Now say the word *burn*. The sounds you hear in *er*, *ir*, and *ur* can all stand for the same vowel sound that you hear in *gerbil*, *bird*, and *turtle*.

gerbil   bird   turtle

 Circle the word that fits in each sentence and has an *e*, *i*, or *u* that makes the same sound you hear in the word *bird*. Then write the word in the blank.

1. The two men _____ climbing Mount Everest.
    went   kept   were

2. People climb because they want _____.
    adventure   risk   prizes

3. Climbing is safer if you do it _____.
    here   together   there

4. Hillary and Norgay were the _____ to reach the top.
    first   tired   paired

 Circle each word that makes the same vowel sound you hear in the word *bird*.

5. Mount Everest is higher than any other mountain.

6. Climbers who go there face the danger of being hurt.

7. It is harder to climb on ice than on dirt.

8. It is safer to circle back if you aren't sure where you are.

Name _____ Date _____

Words, Words, Words

Words with the Same or Opposite Meanings

Synonyms are words that have the same or almost the same meaning. Antonyms are words that have opposite or nearly opposite meanings. If you replace a word in a sentence with a synonym, the meaning does not change. If you replace a word in a sentence with an antonym, the meaning changes.

 Read these sentences. See how the meaning of each sentence changes. This is because the <u>underlined</u> words are antonyms.

Hillary and Norgay wanted to <u>teach</u> more about Mount Everest.

Hillary and Norgay wanted to <u>learn</u> more about Mount Everest.

 Read the sentences. Use a word from the box below to replace each crossed-out word with an antonym. When you are finished, the sentences will tell about a trip to Mount Everest.

1. The expedition to Mount Everest would be ~~safe~~ _____.

2. The climbers knew that it would be ~~short~~ _____

   and ~~easy~~ _____.

3. The climbers were ~~fearful~~ _____ and

   ~~careless~~ _____.

4. The trip would be a ~~failure~~ _____.

careful	success	brave
difficult	long	dangerous

Name _____ Date _____

Strategy: Identifying Cause and Effect

When we read, we think about why things happened and what might happen next. Why something happens is the cause. What happens as a result is the effect. When you read, if you ask yourself questions about *why*, *how*, and *what if*, you are asking yourself questions about causes and effects.

 Read the story below. Think about what happens and why.

> The camp **counselors** wanted the campers to have fun. They planned funny **skits**, many different **crafts**, and canoe races.
>
> The campers left their **campsites** to join the fun. They were **impressed** by the crafts made from clay, wood, and junk. A **totem pole** won first prize. The **canoeists** who won races got awards.
>
> Then the counselors **terrified** the campers with scary skits about monsters in the **wilderness**. The campers **tightened** their hands into fists and closed their eyes. This had been the best night at camp.

 What happened in this story and why? Under *Effect*, write two things that happened in the story. Under *Cause*, explain why they happened.

Cause	◄ ·····►	Effect

Sometimes a story tells you why things happen. Sometimes you have to think on your own about why they might have happened. Either way, you are thinking about causes and effects.

> **Thinking about causes and effects, or asking *why*, *how*, and *what if*, will help you think about what you read.**

Name _____ Date _____

Vocabulary Builder

The words in the box come from the short story you just read. You will see these words again in the story you are about to read.

 Complete each sentence with one of the words. The first one has been done for you.

counselors
impressed
wilderness
skits
crafts
~~totem pole~~
canoeists
campsites
tightened
terrified

1. I am the words ___totem pole___. I am the shape of a tree trunk. I have faces carved into me.

2. I am the word _____. We are the people at camp who teach the campers. We give them games and activities to do.

3. I am the word _____. When you thought something was really cool, then you felt like me.

4. I am the word _____. I am what you did when you wanted someone to feel very afraid.

5. I am the word _____. We are places to stay outside.

6. I am the word _____. I am the opposite of loosened.

7. I am the word _____. We make boats go.

8. I am the word _____. People sometimes call us sketches or short plays.

9. I am the word _____. We are things people make.

10. I am the word _____. I am found far away from cities. The word *wild* is part of me.

Purpose for Reading

Now you are going to read a story. Michael and Tyler are at camp together, but Michael is not feeling very excited. As you read, think about why Michael might not be feeling so excited.

At the Campfire

A flaming arrow flew across the night sky. It hit a large pile of carefully stacked logs. In moments the logs were blazing. Camp Outback's campfire night had begun.

Michael liked the way the **counselors** started the fire. It was cool. But he didn't tell anybody that. After all, he was 13, and this was his third summer at Camp Outback. He had seen the flaming arrow trick before. Plus, he was a city kid from Detroit. City kids didn't say out loud that anything was cool.

"Cool!" said Tyler, who sat next to him.

---

counselors (KOWN suh luhrz) *noun* Counselors are people who teach and help children at camp.

Michael smiled. Tyler was a city kid who was **impressed** by stuff and willing to show it. Michael was only a year older than Tyler, but sometimes Tyler seemed even younger.

Camp Outback was a summer place for Detroit city boys. It was on the shore of East Lake, deep in the **wilderness** of upper Michigan. During the past two summers, Michael had come here for two weeks. He had met Tyler here last year.

Down by the fire, Mr. Bell said, "Welcome to the 'Save Our Lake' campfire." Mr. Bell used to be a Detroit police officer. He ran the camp.

The campfire was in the middle of an outdoor area at the bottom of a hill. Kids sat on log seats cut into the hill like stairs.

Michael and Tyler were sitting high up on the hill. The moon was shining brightly, and they could see East Lake clearly. Michael couldn't make himself look at the water, though.

---

1. Why didn't Michael want to look at the water? Write what you think.

"Get ready!" Mr. Bell said. "We'll have you clapping along to songs about East Lake. Then we'll have some **skits** performed by Cabin B. Finally we'll give out some neat prizes for the best 'Save Our Lake' **crafts**."

---

impressed (ihm PREHSD) *verb* Someone who is impressed likes something or thinks that it is interesting.

wilderness (WIHL duhr nihs) *noun* Wilderness is land where people do not live.

skits (SKIHTS) *noun* Skits are short, funny plays.

crafts (KRAFTS) *noun* Crafts are art and other things made by painting, using clay or wood, or sewing.

Michael rolled his eyes. Saving the lake was important, but this other stuff was boring. Plays, songs, posters, and crafts were not what Michael was all about. "Cool," Tyler whispered. "I hope my **totem pole** wins."

Tyler had made a totem pole out of empty cans. At least Tyler said it was a totem pole. To Michael it looked like cans stuck on a stick.

"We'll announce the 'Save Our Lake' **canoeists** later," Mr. Bell said.

Every summer, campers from Camp Outback teamed up with kids from Wilderness Bay Camp, a nearby girls' camp. Together they cleaned public **campsites** around East Lake. Most kids had to hike to the sites. But the two best canoeists from each camp canoed to campsites far across the lake. Cleaning up trash wasn't much fun, but being picked to canoe to the campsites was a real honor.

2. Why do you think the campsites needed to be cleaned up?

---

totem pole (TOHT uhm POHL) *noun* A totem pole is a post carved and painted with the faces of animals or people.
canoeists (kuh NOO ihsts) *noun* Canoeists are people who ride in small boats called canoes.
campsites (KAMP syts) *noun* Campsites are places where people set up tents.

"Michael, that's us," Tyler whispered. "We're the best canoeists in camp."

"You've got that right," Michael replied. But as he did, his stomach **tightened**. Last year he had wanted to be chosen more than anything. He was a strong swimmer and one of the best canoeists in camp. When he wasn't picked, he was disappointed.

That was last year. Michael had a secret this year. No one at camp knew about it. Everyone thought Michael loved swimming and canoeing. No one noticed that this summer he'd found lots of reasons to skip swimming. In canoeing classes he did well, but he was nervous.

---

3. What do you think caused Michael to skip swimming?

The campfire evening lasted for two hours. Some songs and plays were funny. Some were even silly. Tyler enjoyed them all, but none took Michael's fears away.

When the prizes for best posters and crafts were handed out, Tyler didn't win. He didn't mind, though, because a few minutes later Mr. Bell said something that made him very happy.

Mr. Bell announced in a booming voice, "The 'Save Our Lake' canoeists this year are Tyler McNeill and Michael Cameron."

---

tightened (TYT nd) *verb* Tightened means "became tighter or more firm." If part of a person's body tightened, that person is most likely scared or nervous.

As Tyler yelled, Michael looked fearfully at the lake. He had owned this lake for the last two summers. He'd had no fears. But tomorrow he would have to canoe across it, and the thought **terrified** him.

---

4. Have you ever been terrified? Tell what caused you to be terrified.

---

terrified (TEHR uh fyd) *verb* To have terrified someone is to have made that person very scared.

Name _____ Date _____

Thinking About the Selection

 Fill in the circle of the correct answer.

1. Where are Michael and Tyler from?
   Ⓐ New York City
   Ⓑ Detroit
   Ⓒ the shore of East Lake
   Ⓓ the wilderness of upper Michigan

2. How do Michael and Tyler know each other?
   Ⓐ They met in Detroit.   Ⓒ They met at camp.
   Ⓑ They go to school together.   Ⓓ They are brothers.

3. What is Michael's secret?
   Ⓐ He has been practicing swimming and canoeing.
   Ⓑ He has become scared of swimming and canoeing.
   Ⓒ He does not really know how to swim.
   Ⓓ He likes making arts and crafts at camp.

4. What will the boys chosen as "Save Our Lake" canoeists do?
   Ⓐ They will canoe across the lake and clean up campsites.
   Ⓑ They will teach canoeing at the girls' camp.
   Ⓒ They will go on a week-long canoe trip around the lake.
   Ⓓ They will win a free canoe to take home after camp.

5. Contrast Michael and Tyler. What is one way they are different?

   _____

   _____

6. Why do you think Michael is not as excited as Tyler about being

   chosen to be a canoeist? _____

   _____

Name _____ Date _____

Prewriting

Planning Chart

In "At the Campfire," Michael was picked as a "Save Our Lake" canoeist. He was chosen because he was a great swimmer and canoeist. Even though he was nervous, he could do a good job. Think of a job at your school that you would do well. Think of why you should have it.

 Fill in the chart below. Tell about a job at your school that you would be good at. Tell why you would be good at it. Give an example of how you are responsible. This will help to show why you should get the job.

A job I would be good at:

Why I would be good at it:

1.

2.

3.

I can be counted on. An example of how I am responsible is:

Filling out this page will help you organize your ideas before you start writing.

Name _____ Date _____

A Plan for Writing

Pick Me!

A business letter is written to do or get something. It has all of the parts below.

 Write a business letter to your school principal. Tell why you should have a job at your school. Use ideas from your chart.

Today's Date >	_____
Principal's Name *Your School* *School Address* >	_____ _____ _____
Greeting: >	Dear _____,
Body Paragraph 1: *Tell what job or role you want.* >	I am writing because I would like to _____ _____ at our school. This letter tells why I think I would be good at this job.
Body Paragraph 2: *Tell why you would be good.* >	I would be good because _____ _____.
Body Paragraph 3: *Tell how you are responsible.* >	The school could count on me in this role. An example of how I am responsible is _____ _____.
	Sincerely,
Sign your name: >	_____

Writing

 Write a letter telling why you should have a job at your school. Use the plan above to help you. Write your letter on a sheet of paper.

Name _____ Date _____

Breaking the Code

R-controlled vowels *ar* and *or*

When the letter *r* follows a vowel, the vowel is neither short nor long. The vowel has its own sound. Say the word **at**. Now say the word **art**. Do you hear the difference? Say the word **cod**. Now say the word **cord**. The sounds you hear in **ar** and **or** can stand for the vowel sounds in the words *car*, *corn*, *worm*, and *square*.

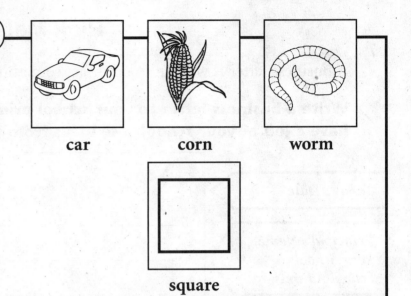

car   corn   worm

square

 Circle the word that fits in each sentence and has the letter *a* or the letter *o* whose sound has changed because of the letter *r*. Then write the word in the blank.

1. A skit is a _____ play.   **yarn   barn   short**

2. Actors _____ in a skit.   **starve   perform   explore**

3. Being chosen is a real _____.   **honor   score   charm**

4. Water made Michael feel _____.   **sore   bored   scared**

 Choose a word from the box below. Write it on the blank beside the word that has the same sound of *or* or *ar*.

story   worm   start   care

5. share _____

6. large _____

7. torn _____

8. word _____

Name _____   Date _____

Words, Words, Words

Homonyms

Some words sound the same but are different. You might like to take a trip to **see** the **sea**. **See** and **sea** sound the same, but they have different spellings and meanings. These words are called *homonyms*. You can tell what a word means by the context, or the words around that word.

 Each pair of sentences below has two words that sound the same but have different meanings and spellings. Circle these words.

Michael was chosen for the "Save the Lake" canoe trip.
He was one of four campers who were chosen.

• •

You don't sail a canoe; you paddle it.
I have never seen a canoe for sale in the city.

 Now write your own sentences using homonyms.

ate (it has to do with food) and **eight** (the number)

1. ate _____

2. eight _____

know (after you have learned something) and **no** (the opposite of yes)

3. know _____

4. no _____

would (a form of will) and **wood** (what a tree is made of)

5. would _____

6. wood _____

Reading Workout Book 2, SV 9781419099052

Name _____ Date _____

Strategy: Identifying Cause and Effect

For most events, we can think of causes, or reasons why things happen. Why something happens is the cause. What happens as a result is the effect. We can usually see how an event causes another event. When you read, words like *so*, *because*, *if*, and *then* are often clues that the author is telling about causes and effects.

 Read the passage below. Think about what happens and why.

Trash is a problem in the United States. This is because people in the United States **discard tons** of trash every day. Some trash falls to the ground as litter. Other trash goes into **refuse bins**. Then it goes to an **incinerator** or a **landfill**. Some landfills cover **acres** of land because there is so much trash.

This trash causes problems for our **society**. If the wrong things are thrown away, trash then becomes **poisonous**. Some landfills make a gas called **methane**. This gas **pollutes** the air.

 Read the chart. The left side lists trash problems, or effects of trash. The middle has a clue word from the story. This clue will help you find the cause of the problem. Write the cause in the right side of the chart.

Trash Problems (Effects)	Clue Word	Cause of the Problem
Trash is a problem in the United States	because	
Landfills cover acres	because	
Trash can be poisonous	if	

Thinking about causes helps you understand problems. When you know why a problem happens, you can help solve the problem!

Name _____ Date _____

Vocabulary Builder

The words in the box come from the passage you just read. You will see these words again in the passage you are about to read.

➡️ **Choose a word from the box to complete each sentence. Write the letters of the word on the blanks. The first word has been done for you. When you are finished, the letters in the circles will make a sentence. This sentence is a message to you about the trash problem.**

discard
~~society~~
tons
refuse bins
landfill
acres
incinerator
poisonous
methane
pollutes

(1) People living together in a large group, such as a country, are called a s o c i e t (y) .

(2) We measure something really heavy in __ O__ __ .

(3) Containers that hold our trash are called __ __ __ O__ __ __ __ __ __ .

(4) You __ __ __ O__ __ __ trash when you throw it away.

(5) Trash can be burned in an __ __ __ __ __ __ __ O__ __ __ .

(6) Trash can be buried in a __ __ O__ __ __ __ __ .

(7) __ __ __ O__ __ __ __ is a gas that is made by trash.

(8) We measure large pieces of land in __ __ __ O__ .

(9) When something makes things dirty, it __ __ __ O__ __ __ __ them.

(10) Something O__ __ __ __ __ __ __ __ can harm people and animals.

Answer: __ __ __   __ __ __   __ __ __ __ .

Purpose for Reading

Now you will read about the trash problem in the United States. People of the United States make a lot of trash. Read to learn where it comes from and where it goes.

Throw It Away

It's called garbage, waste, litter, and junk. It's made up of food, paper, plastic, metal, cloth, and glass. It's trash, and it's everywhere.

Trash is anything that we throw away. It can be as small as a bottle cap or as large as a refrigerator. Trash can be found floating in space or bobbing on the ocean waves.

People in the United States throw out the most trash in the world. We each **discard** about four pounds every day. That's enough trash to fill sixty-three thousand garbage trucks!

Today, people want the latest and the newest things. Ads on TV and the radio say "buy, buy, buy."

discard (dihs KAHRD) *verb* To discard is to get rid of.

Name _____ Date _____

> **1. Why do you think there is so much trash in the United States?**

Everyone wants the fastest computer and the largest TV. If something breaks, people often throw it out and buy a new one. All this makes the United States a "throw away" **society**.

Each year U.S. citizens throw away two hundred million tires. Each day about twenty thousand TVs are tossed out in the United States. The people of New York City make about twenty-five thousand **tons** of trash each day. Where does all this trash go?

---

society (suh SY uh tee) *noun* Society means "all the people living together in a group."
tons (TUHNZ) *noun* Tons are measures of weight. One ton equals two thousand pounds.

Unit 1: Trash with Dash
Reading Workout Book 2, SV 9781419099052

The Trash Trail

The trash trail starts in homes, offices, factories, and stores. People throw food, empty boxes, and other junk into trash cans. The cans are emptied into **refuse bins**. They're also put out for garbage workers to collect.

A garbage truck holds five to seven tons of trash. A city as big as New York City has about one thousand garbage trucks.

Most garbage trucks take the trash to a **landfill**. The trash is buried. In New York City, garbage trucks dump the trash onto boats. The boats take the trash to Fresh Kills Landfill on Staten Island. At the landfill, bulldozers cover the trash with dirt.

Many landfills become mountains of trash. Fresh Kills is the world's largest landfill. It covers three thousand **acres** of land, and it's about five hundred feet high. That's twice as tall as the Statue of Liberty!

Some trash might be burned in an **incinerator**. The trash turns into ash, which is usually buried in a landfill.

---

2. What do you think happens to landfills after a while?

---

refuse bins (rih FYOOZ bihnz) *noun* Refuse bins are large metal boxes or bins that hold garbage.

landfill (LAND fihl) *noun* A landfill is a place where trash is buried.

acres (AY kuhrz) *noun* Acres are measures of land. One acre of land is equal to 43,560 square feet.

incinerator (ihn SIHN uhr ayt uhr) *noun* An incinerator is a place where trash and waste are burned and turned into ashes.

The Trouble with Trash

Landfills cover trash and keep it from smelling, but landfills have many problems. Every day, people throw away cans of old paint, cleaners, and sprays. These cans may still have **poisonous** materials such as lead in them. If these materials mix with rain, they can make poison. The poison can get into drinking water and rivers. New landfills pump out the poison, but there is still a problem with where to dump it.

Trash buried in landfills also makes a gas called **methane**. Methane is not a poison, but it **pollutes** the air and can catch on fire easily. In new landfills, pipes hold the gas until it can be burned safely. Most older landfills do not have these pipes, though.

One of the biggest problems with trash is where to put new landfills. Most people don't want landfills built near their homes. They don't want the smell, the mess, and the problems with poisons and methane. Yet old landfills are closing because they aren't safe or because they're full.

---

3. What do you think is the biggest problem caused by so much trash?

---

poisonous (POY zuh nuhs) *adjective* Poisonous means "able to make animals or people sick."
methane (MEHTH ayn) *noun* Methane is a gas that can catch on fire. It has no color or smell.
pollutes (puh LOOTS) *verb* Something that pollutes makes other things dirty.

Some U.S. cities send trash to other states. In 1998, Virginia took in over 3 million tons of trash. One boat from New York City traveled 162 days to find a place to dump its trash. None of the states it visited would take its 3,169 tons of trash. So the boat came back to New York City, where the trash was burned in an incinerator.

People will continue to make trash. Soon there will not be many places to put it. There are ways we can all help solve the problem of what to do with our waste.

4. **What are some ways you can think of to help solve the problem of trash?**

Name _____   Date _____

Thinking About the Selection

 Fill in the circle of the correct answer.

1 Which of the following is a place to put trash?
Ⓐ garbage   Ⓒ litter
Ⓑ waste   Ⓓ refuse bin

2 This passage is mostly about—
Ⓐ where trash comes from and where it goes.
Ⓑ how we can solve the problem of trash.
Ⓒ what people will do with trash in the future.
Ⓓ how trash is different around the world.

3 What is one reason that landfills are covered with dirt?
Ⓐ Dirt keeps landfills from smelling too bad.
Ⓑ Dirt gets rid of poisonous gases.
Ⓒ Dirt stops methane gas from being made.
Ⓓ Dirt protects water that is close to the landfills.

4 Why did the author probably write this passage?
Ⓐ to compare trash in the past with trash today
Ⓑ to make city planners think they shouldn't build new landfills
Ⓒ to tell readers about the problem of trash
Ⓓ to tell readers not to worry about trash

5 What is one reason people in the United States make so much trash?

_____

_____

6 What are two problems caused by trash?

_____

_____

Prewriting

Idea Chart

"Throw It Away" tells about how people in the United States buy and throw out a lot of things. It also tells about the problems caused by all of the trash. To solve the problems, people need to realize how much they buy and throw away.

 Fill out the chart below. List all of the things you have bought recently. Also list all of the things you have put in the garbage. Then, under each list, circle the types of things you listed. You can also write the names of other types that aren't given. Finally, answer the question below.

Types of Things I Have Bought		Types of Things I Have Thrown Out	
_____	_____	_____	_____
_____	_____	_____	_____
_____	_____	_____	_____
_____	_____	_____	_____

Types of Things I Have Bought		Types of Things I Have Thrown Out	
clothing		clothing	metal
food		plastic	food waste
sports supplies		glass	yard waste
paper products		paper	other types:
other types:			

Do you think you make a lot of garbage?   yes   no

Name _____ Date _____

A Plan for Writing

The Sum of All Trash

A summary gives general information. It tells only the main or important things.
It does not have many details.

 **Write a summary of the trash you make. Use the ideas from your chart.
Tell about the things you buy and throw away. Give the types of things
and a few examples.**

Introduction	There is too much trash. Trash is caused by _____ _____. One way to fight waste is _____.
What you buy	I buy things. The types of things I buy are _____ _____. For example, some things I have bought lately are _____.
What you throw away	I throw things away. The types of things I put in the garbage are _____. For example, some things I have thrown away recently are _____.
How much you waste	I think that I *do / do not* (circle one) make a lot of garbage. I think this because _____ _____.

Writing

 **Write a summary about the garbage you make. Tell about the kinds of
things you buy and throw away. Give just a few details. Write your
summary on a separate sheet of paper.**

Reading Workout Book 2, SV 9781419099052

Name _____ Date _____

Breaking the Code

Sounds of *oo*

The letters *oo* can stand for the sound you hear in *hook*. You can hear this sound in *book*, *wood*, and *foot*. The letters *oo* can also stand for the sound you hear in *zoo*. This is the sound you hear in *moon*, *balloon*, and *spool*.

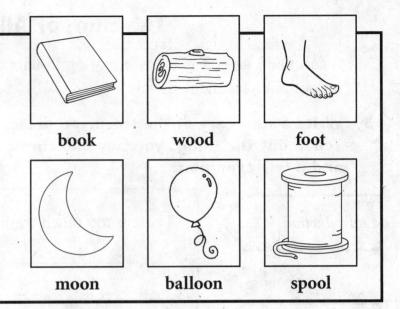

book   wood   foot

moon   balloon   spool

Circle the word with the *oo* sound in *hook* that fits in each sentence. Then write the word in the blank.

1. This passage takes a _____ at trash.   **broom   look   zoom**

2. Trash is a problem in our _____.
   school   room   neighborhood

Underline the word with the *oo* sound in *zoo* that fits in each sentence. Then write the word in the blank.

3. A lot of trash comes from _____.   **wood   cook   food**

4. We are running out of _____ for trash.   **wool   room   goods**

Circle each word with the *oo* sound in *hook*. Underline each word with the *oo* sound in *zoo*.

5. We need to solve the trash problem soon.

6. It is time we took a look at the problem.

7. It might be good to use less paper at school.

8. That would save wood, too.

Words, Words, Words

Context Clues

Good readers use context clues. These are words in a story that can help you figure out a new word's meaning. Context clues might be words in the same sentence as the new word. Context clues might also be in the sentences before and after the word.

 Read the following sentences. Then match each <u>underlined</u> word to its definition. Tell what context clues helped you learn each word's meaning.

- Trash is a big problem. People throw away trash that is not safe. It is bad for people and the environment. This kind of trash is called <u>hazardous</u> waste.

- We need to <u>minimize</u> the amount of trash we make. If we can make less trash, that will help the environment.

- One other way to help the problem of trash is to <u>recycle</u>. We can make old bottles into new glass. We can make old paper into clean paper.

 Match each word with its meaning. Write the letter of the definition next to the word.

1. hazardous _____   **a.** to make smaller or less

2. minimize _____   **b.** to turn trash into something new

3. recycle _____   **c.** dangerous

 Tell what words were context clues. The first one has been done for you.

Word	Context Clues
hazardous	*trash that is not safe*
minimize	
recycle	

Count on Me—Wrap-Up

Guarding the Vikings®

My brother Ted is 20, but he still lives at home.

"The food's cheaper," he says.

Actually, the food is free. Free food is important to Ted because he needs to save all of his money to pay for college. He goes to school full time and has two part-time jobs. Ted's main job is at a sporting goods store. He stocks shelves, helps customers, and runs the checkout. When he isn't at the store or at school, Ted works as a security guard. He usually covers big events such as concerts. A couple of months ago, he told me that he was working at a new kind of show.

"Mr. Riley has had the best guard job in the city for 35 years," Ted said, "but soon he and his wife are moving away. Now I have Mr. Riley's prize job— guarding the Vikings."

My mouth dropped open.

"Not only do I guard them," Ted said, "I am right down there on the field with them."

My eyes bugged out.

"You get paid for that?" I asked.

---

1. What do you think Ted's brother meant when he said, "My eyes bugged out"?

Ted nodded. He had a grin on his face the size of Alaska.

Ted and I love the Vikings. We live in St. Paul, and the Vikings are our city's football team. As long as I can remember, I've wanted to go to a Vikings game.

"We can't afford it," Dad would always say.

I quit asking a long time ago. Now that I know how much the tickets cost, I think Dad was right. Anyway, I figured this was my best chance to see my team up close.

"Can you get me into a game?" I asked Ted.

2. How did Ted's brother think Ted might get him into the game? How is that different from the usual way of getting into a game?

"No," he said.

"But you're their guard. You're right there on the field with them."

Ted just looked at me and chewed. He was eating a huge sandwich for lunch. When he finished, he said, "I'm not on the team. I just watch the field."

"But you know the players," I said.

"Sure, I know them, but that doesn't mean they know me." He took another bite and chewed slowly.

"Well, don't they have tickets? Can't they give you one or two?"

"We're not exactly best friends," Ted said. "They're in the football league. I'm in the guard league."

I wasn't about to give up. "Just see what you can do," I said.

Ted finished his lunch and stood up to leave.

"Remember your poor little brother!" I yelled after him as he headed out the door.

He didn't even turn around.

Name _____   Date _____

3. Do you think Ted will be able to get tickets for his brother? Tell why you think he will or will not.

Weeks went by, and I didn't get any free tickets. I bugged Ted every chance I got, but it didn't seem to do any good. I was beginning to wonder if he really did guard the Vikings. I looked for Ted every time they showed a home game on TV, but I never saw him.

"So why haven't you been on TV?" I asked one day.

"Who wants to see a guard standing around?" Ted answered.

He had a good point.

• • • • • • • • • • • • • • • •

I was almost ready to give up, when I got lucky. I was getting dressed for school one day and listening to the radio. The DJ was running a contest. If you called in first with the right answer to his question, you won a pair of tickets to the next Vikings home game. The DJ played three notes of a song and said, "If you know this song, call us NOW."

I was amazed. He was playing my mom's favorite song, "American Pie." I called the number right away, and the DJ answered on the first ring.

"Good morning. What's the song?" he asked.

"'American Pie!'" I yelled.

"You got it!" he said.

I couldn't believe it. I'd won two tickets to the Vikings game!

• • • • • • • • • • • • • • • •

The big day finally arrived. My friend John and I got to the field about an hour early. Not many people were in the stands yet. I looked all over the field for Ted, but I didn't see him.

I was starting to think he really didn't work there when I spotted him. The game was about to begin, and the teams were coming out of the tunnels. Suddenly a guard came out of the Vikings' tunnel. It was Ted! He stood to the side while the players ran out. Then, when the team was on the field, he turned around and stood facing the tunnel.

While I watched the game, I kept **glancing at** Ted. I never saw him turn his head. He spent the whole game looking down the tunnel, away from the field.

The Vikings won, and the crowd went wild. I stayed until the very end to watch the players leave the field. Ted was still there, guarding the tunnel as each one passed by.

I got home before Ted did after the game. When he walked into the house, it was hard for me not to grin.

"I saw you today," I said.

"It was a good game, wasn't it?" he asked.

I couldn't help it. I started laughing. "How would you know?" I asked.

"I've got ears," Ted said.

"I didn't once see you look at the game," I chuckled.

"I'm not supposed to," Ted said. "I'm there to guard the team."

"Doesn't it drive you crazy, not being able to watch?" I asked.

"No," he said. "I'm helping my team. I'm there with them, and I'm earning money at the same time. It's the best job in the world."

I quit laughing. He was right.

---

4. How does what you thought Ted did while he was guarding the Vikings compare with what Ted actually did at the games?

Name _____ Date _____

Count on Me—Wrap-Up

 Fill in the circle of the correct answer.

1. Why is Ted's job as a guard interesting?
   Ⓐ He becomes good friends with football players.
   Ⓑ He gets to go to football games and support the team.
   Ⓒ He gets free tickets for his friends for games and concerts.
   Ⓓ He gets to play different kinds of sports and games.

2. The words *glancing at* in this story mean—
   Ⓐ looking at.   Ⓒ moving from.
   Ⓑ walking by.   Ⓓ sitting beside.

3. Why didn't Ted watch the game?
   Ⓐ He was not interested.
   Ⓑ He was busy working.
   Ⓒ He was talking to his brother.
   Ⓓ He was working at the sports store.

4. How does Ted feel about his job for the Vikings?
   Ⓐ proud   Ⓒ worried
   Ⓑ bored   Ⓓ unimportant

5. What is one way that Ted's day at the football game was like his brother's day? What is one way that it was different?

   _____

   _____

   _____

6. What lesson could you learn from this story? Give examples from the story to support your answer.

   _____

   _____

   _____

www.harcourtschoolsupply.com   **60**

Unit 1: Count On Me—Wrap-Up
Reading Workout Book 2, SV 9781419099052

Count on Me—Wrap-Up

Long Ride into History

Hundreds of men marched through the night. Their horses had already died. Now icy winds poked the men's bodies like needles. Sharp rocks cut through the bottoms of their shoes. The men struggled to stay on their bloody feet. They dreamed of hot coffee, bacon, and fresh bread, but they would not find these treats waiting for them at the end of their journey.

1. What do you think has happened to these men?

Back at their camp, they drank cold, bitter coffee and ate hard, sour bread. Instead of bacon, they had gray salt pork that had not been cooked enough. They slept in run-down cabins on cots covered with bugs. They had no way to take a bath. Many became ill from the dirty conditions.

These brave men were the first African American soldiers in the regular U.S. Army. They joined the army after the Civil War. They were called "Buffalo Soldiers."

2. Why do you think these men were the first African American soldiers?

Because of the Civil War, slavery ended in the United States in 1863. African Americans who had been slaves before the war were set free. They hoped they would be treated fairly. Many white people in the country still thought of African American people as slaves. The story of the Buffalo Soldiers is an example of this kind of **prejudice**. The Buffalo Soldiers were often treated differently because they were African American.

The Buffalo Soldiers made up one-fifth of the army's soldiers in the western United States. After the Civil War, the United States sent many of its soldiers out west. These men helped to open up land for people coming from the East.

Before joining the army, most of the Buffalo Soldiers were not fighters or explorers. Most of them came from cities and farms in the East. Some of the men had worked as bakers, cooks, or farmers. Some were freed slaves. Others had been painters or cattle drivers. They were as young as 18. Many Buffalo Soldiers could not even read or write. They had to go to school at night for extra training, even after they had worked all day.

Being a Buffalo Soldier was hard work. Buffalo Soldiers worked seven days a week. Their only holidays were Christmas and the Fourth of July. They often traveled for six months and covered more than 1,000 miles. A lack of water and bad weather added to their problems. They had to promise to stay in the army for at least 5 years. Most of them earned only $13 a month.

3. Why do you think these men became Buffalo Soldiers?

As U.S. soldiers, these young African American men often fought against Native Americans. They helped the army capture Native Americans such as Cochise and Geronimo. Even though they often fought against the Buffalo Soldiers, Native Americans thought they were very brave. In fact, Native Americans were the first people to call the men Buffalo Soldiers. Their fighting spirit made the Native Americans think of buffaloes. Native Americans had great respect for how strong buffaloes were. The name Buffalo Soldier was an honor. The Buffalo Soldiers liked this name and put it on their company's coat of arms.

The Buffalo Soldiers fought in the Spanish-American War in Cuba. Cuba wanted to be free from Spain. The United States decided to help Cuba. The Buffalo Soldiers joined Teddy Roosevelt, who would later become President of the United States. He, his Rough Riders, and the Buffalo Soldiers charged up San Juan Hill. The Rough Riders were Roosevelt's soldiers on horses. The battle in Cuba was the first time that black soldiers and white soldiers fought side by side.

Even though their first job was to fight, the Buffalo Soldiers did much more to help the United States. They also guarded people and railroad workers moving west. They tracked people who stole cattle and horses. They guarded mail stations. They carried the mail when no one else could get it through. They opened three hundred miles of new roads and made maps for the new country. They saved the lives of settlers by leading them to water. Their courage and hard work helped make the West a safer place for new settlers.

4. What do you think was the most important thing that the Buffalo Soldiers did? Explain why you think so.

The Buffalo Soldiers worked hard for many years to help their country and keep it safe. Sixty-eight thousand of them were killed, hurt, or listed as missing. Eighteen won the Medal of Honor. Thirteen were Buffalo Soldiers for more than 25 years.

For a long time, though, no one recognized their work. Finally, in 1992, the United States rewarded the bravery of the Buffalo Soldiers. On July 26, they were honored with a monument at Fort Leavenworth, Kansas.

General Colin Powell spoke at the ceremony, and he said that the Buffalo Soldiers always knew that hate could not destroy them. They fought hard for their country because they believed their pain and loss would help end prejudice. On April 22, 1994, the post office brought out a new stamp. The stamp honored the daring and bravery of the Buffalo Soldiers. They were the last men on horses in the United States Army. The monument and the stamp helped the Buffalo Soldiers ride into their proper place in history.

Count on Me—Wrap-Up

 Fill in the circle of the correct answer.

1. This passage is mostly about—
   Ⓐ the events that led up to the Civil War.
   Ⓑ the importance of the Buffalo Soldiers.
   Ⓒ why learning U.S. history is important.
   Ⓓ how the American West was settled.

2. The word *prejudice* in this passage means a—
   Ⓐ bad opinion without a good reason.
   Ⓑ way of treating all people as equals.
   Ⓒ group of people respected for no reason.
   Ⓓ time in history about which people forget.

3. Many Buffalo Soldiers were sent out west because—
   Ⓐ the army did not think they should fight in important battles.
   Ⓑ the army wanted the black and white armies to stay separate.
   Ⓒ they wanted to leave the Eastern and Southern United States.
   Ⓓ there were many jobs to be done to help people settle the West.

4. Colin Powell said that the Buffalo Soldiers fought for the United States so that they would—
   Ⓐ help the North win the Civil War over the South.
   Ⓑ help end prejudice against African Americans.
   Ⓒ be honored with a stamp and monument.
   Ⓓ be paid a lot of money in the army.

5. The Buffalo Soldiers were strong fighters. How else did they help the United States?

   _____

   _____

   _____

Unit 2

DO THE RIGHT THING

Doing what is right means being honest with others and with yourself. It means taking a stand against what you know is wrong. Read the problems below. Think about the right thing to do for each problem. Then write your ideas in the boxes.

The Right Thing to Do

When a friend needs help but won't ask for it—	When you want something, but you don't have the money—
When a bully picks on a friend—	When someone else gets blamed for something you did—

Think About It!

Describe a time when you did the right thing even though it wasn't easy. What did you do?

What happened because of what you did?

Why was it the right thing to do?

Name _____ Date _____

Strategy: Making Inferences, Drawing Conclusions

Sometimes when you read, you figure out information that is not written in the story. This is called making inferences or drawing conclusions. Read the sentence "Pete barks and digs for a bone." You can draw the conclusion that Pete is a dog and not a person. You know that Pete is a dog because of the details about what he does. You also know because of your own experiences with dogs. When you read, you make inferences by using details and your own experiences.

 Read the story below. Then make an inference or draw a conclusion about where this story takes place.

> We **recited** the class rules. "**Respect** others. **Communicate** with others."
>
> We started writing, but paper was **scarce**. "Who has been **raiding** the paper?" our teacher asked. There was no **reaction** from the students.
>
> "Ask **permission** before taking paper. I don't want to have to **contact** the **authorities**," she joked.
>
> The class heard a **hiccup**. "I took it," Jess said. "I needed it for a project. I'll bring more tomorrow."
>
> "You are excused," our teacher said, smiling. "Tell us about your project."

 Where does this story take place? Write what you think. Then tell what details made you draw this conclusion.

This story takes place _____.

These details from the story made me think this.

1. _____

2. _____

> **If you think about more than just what is written in the story, you will become a better reader.**

Vocabulary Builder

recited ~~recited~~
communicate
scarce
hiccup
raiding
reaction
permission
contact
respect
authorities

The words in the box come from the story you just read. You will see the words again in the story you are about to read.

 Write the correct word in each blank. This will help you think about each word's meaning. The first one is done for you.

① He _____recited_____ the words, saying them over and over again.

② His father told him to _____ and honor older people.

③ Bill's mom caught him _____ the cookie jar.

④ They spoke different languages. It was hard to _____.

⑤ Food was _____. There was not enough for everyone.

⑥ She was happy about the news. You could tell by her _____.

⑦ You can go only if you ask for _____ first.

⑧ A funny sound that your throat makes is called a _____.

⑨ To _____ a person means to find the person and talk.

⑩ Her purse was stolen. She called the _____.

Purpose for Reading

Now you are going to read about a strange place. Everyone there is alike until someone different arrives. Read to find out what happens. Think about what it would be like to live in this place.

A Zog on the Pod!

This morning began like every other morning. When I woke up, I joined my family in the common room. Together we **recited** the Pod Rules:

"Always remember the good of the Pod.

The Pod feeds the Pod, and the Pod helps the Pod.

Secrets hurt the Pod, and strangers hurt the Pod.

The Pod is all for one, and the Pod is one for all."

Then I hurried into the garden to pick bread berries for breakfast.

The purple sky of planet Tolup was clear. The twin orange suns blazed like monsters' eyes.

recited (rih SYT ehd) *verb* Recited means "said out loud from memory."

Reading Workout Book 2, SV 9781419099052

When I heard a familiar flapping sound, I turned and smiled. It was my pet Potok, Gova. He flew across the garden and landed on my shoulder. I ran my hand over Gova's soft, orange feathers. His long, purple beak hooked over his blue grin.

"Good morning, Sasha," Gova thought.

"Good morning, Gova," I thought back.

Gova and I don't **communicate** by talking. When we want to share our thoughts, I can "hear" his, and he can "hear" mine.

"I'm flying off now," Gova told me.

"Have a nice trip around the Pod," I answered.

After Gova flew away, I turned back to the bread berry bush. I was careful not to drop any berries, because food on our Pod is so **scarce**. We need every last berry we can find.

> **1. What do you think a Pod is? Tell why you think so.**

Just then, I heard a sound like a **hiccup**. It came from the round tent where my parents keep our garden tools and seeds. I figured some animal must be **raiding** our seeds, so I raced toward the tent, shouting.

---

communicate (kuh MYOO nih kayt) *verb* To communicate is to share information with someone.
scarce (SKEHRS) *adjective* Something that is scarce is rare or in low supply.
hiccup (HIHK uhp) *noun* A hiccup is a short, sharp breath that makes a small sound.
raiding (RAYD ihng) *verb* Someone who is raiding a place is going to steal something.

But when I stepped through the tent's flap, I saw a very strange boy curled up in the corner. He had red eyes, green skin, and a pointy nose. His long ears poked out from his head.

My own hair is blue, and my eyes are yellow, the same as the others on my Pod. That's how I knew right away that he was a Zog. I had never seen one before.

> **2. How do you think Sasha will react to the Zog?**

My first **reaction** was to jump back. But the boy called out, "Help me!"

His words stopped me cold. The boy sounded the same as everyone on my Pod!

"You're a Zog, aren't you?" I asked. The boy nodded.

I'd heard about the Zogs. They owned tiny farms outside the Pods of Eastland, where I lived. The Rulers of Eastland hated the Zogs. The Rulers had forced the Zogs to give up most of their crops. Many Zogs were now starving.

"I'm so hungry!" the Zog cried out.

I knew I shouldn't feed the boy without **permission**, but he looked so thin. I took out a handful of bread berries and set them on a flat stone that my father uses to grind seeds.

"My name is Sasha," I said.

"I'm Jared," he answered. He finished the berries in a breath.

---

reaction (ree AK shuhn) *noun* A reaction is an action that is done in answer to another action.
permission (puhr MIHSH uhn) *noun* Permission is the act of letting someone do something.

3. Why do you think Sasha gave the berries to the Zog?

"Where are your parents?" I asked him.

"I don't know!" he replied. "Last night, we were trying to cross your Pod. We thought a Pod girl had seen us, and we got scared. When we ran to hide, I got lost. My parents told me to find the Pod of Goodell if we ever got separated. Will you help me **contact** Goodell?"

contact (KAHN takt) *verb* To contact someone is to talk to or send a message to that person.

The Rules of the Pod demanded that I say no. I had heard of a Pod that had helped some Zogs once. When the Rulers found out, they broke up the Pod and took over the land. Without land to grow food on, many of those Pod folk died.

My parents had taught me to **respect** the Rules of the Pod. But they also had taught me to treat others as I would like to be treated. Did they mean Zogs, too?

"Wait for me here, Jared," I said. "I'll be back as soon as I can."

I knew I'd be back. What I hadn't decided was whether I'd bring the **authorities**.

---

4. Do you think Sasha will tell everyone about Jared? Tell why you think so.

---

respect (rih SPEHKT) *verb* To respect the rules is to follow them.
authorities (uh THAWR uh teez) *noun* The authorities are the people in charge.

Name _____ Date _____

Thinking About the Selection

 Fill in the circle of the correct answer.

1. Which of the following is <u>not</u> a Pod rule?
   - Ⓐ The Pod helps the Pod.
   - Ⓒ Strangers hurt the Pod.
   - Ⓑ Different people help the Pod.
   - Ⓓ The Pod is one for all.

2. How does Sasha find Jared?
   - Ⓐ Her sister tells her Jared is there.
   - Ⓑ The police come to get him.
   - Ⓒ He makes a sound in the round tent.
   - Ⓓ He has stolen all of the family's food.

3. How does Sasha know Jared is different from her?
   - Ⓐ He speaks differently.
   - Ⓒ He is dressed differently.
   - Ⓑ He looks different.
   - Ⓓ He eats different food.

4. Why is Jared in Sasha's Pod?
   - Ⓐ He wants to live in the Pod.
   - Ⓑ He wants to meet Sasha.
   - Ⓒ He came to steal food.
   - Ⓓ He is looking for the Pod of Goodell.

5. How did you know this story does not take place on Earth? Name two reasons.

   _____

   _____

6. Do you think Sasha will tell the authorities about Jared? Tell what makes you think that.

   _____

   _____

Prewriting

Idea Chart

In "A Zog on the Pod!" Sasha has to decide if she will help Jared. She might go to the Rulers of Eastland to ask them to help Jared. Think about someone you know who has been in trouble or needed help. How would you ask the authorities to help that person?

➡ **Fill in the chart below. Tell about the person in trouble. Tell why that person should be helped.**

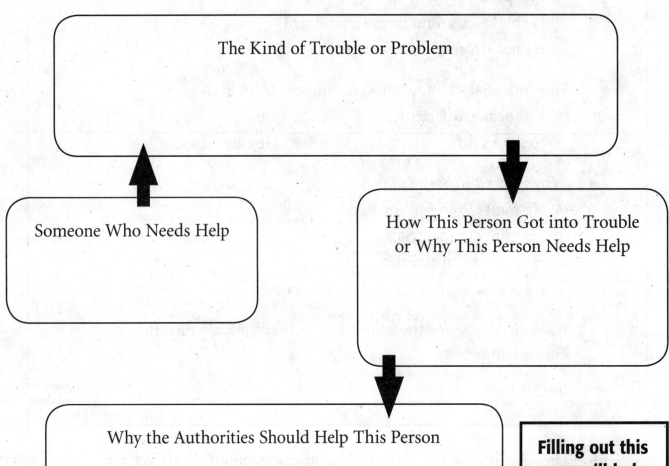

The Kind of Trouble or Problem

Someone Who Needs Help

How This Person Got into Trouble or Why This Person Needs Help

Why the Authorities Should Help This Person

1.

2.

3.

Filling out this page will help you organize your ideas before you start writing.

Name _____ Date _____

A Plan for Writing

Saving Someone

A speech is spoken to a crowd. A speech tells people about someone or something. Often it tries to get people to think in a certain way or do something. A speech must give good reasons to change people's thoughts or make them take action.

 Write a speech to get help for someone. Use the ideas from your chart.

> **Tell people why you are speaking.**

> **Tell about the person's problem.**

> **Give three reasons why this person needs help.**

Ladies and Gentlemen! I am here today to ask you to help

_____. I ask you to help _____ because

_____.

This person needs help because _____

_____

_____.

Here is why you should help this person. First _____

_____.

Also _____

_____.

Finally _____

_____.

Writing

 Write a speech to get the authorities to help someone. Use the plan above to help you. Tell the authorities why they should help the person. Give three good reasons. You can add more details, but follow the order of your plan. Write your speech on a separate sheet of paper.

Breaking the Code

Sounds of *ow*

The letters *ow* can stand for the sound that you hear in the word *cow*. You can hear this sound in *crown*, *owl*, and *eyebrow*. The letters *ow* can also stand for the **long o** sound you hear in the word *crow*. This is the sound you hear in *row*, *bowl*, and *pillow*.

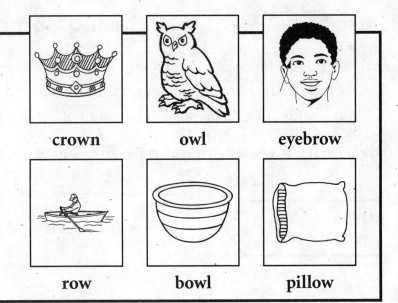

crown owl eyebrow

row bowl pillow

 Circle the word with the *ow* sound in *cow* that fits in each sentence. Then write the word in the blank.

1. Sasha found Jared _____ in the   **below down slow** round tent.

2. Sasha is not _____ to feed Jared.   **allowed known owned**

 Underline the word with the *ow* sound in *crow* that fits in each sentence. Then write the word in the blank.

3. Sasha did not _____ what to do.   **how know down**

4. Jared's family cannot _____   **plow flower grow** food, so they are hungry.

 Circle each word with the *ow* sound in *cow*. Underline each word with the *ow* sound in *crow*.

5. Sasha's own hair is blue, and her eyes are yellow.

6. That is how she knows Jared is different.

7. Jared frowns as he tells her that his people are now starving.

8. Jared must not show himself to anyone.

www.harcourtschoolsupply.com **78** Unit 2: Saving the Zog
  Reading Workout Book 2, SV 9781419099052

Words, Words, Words

Understanding Words with
More Than One Meaning

Some words have more than one meaning. The word *pet* has more than one meaning. **Pet** can mean:

a. to pat   **b.** an animal that is kept or cared for

 Read the two sentences below. Then circle the letter that goes with the meaning for *pet* as it is used in each sentence.

1. It was my **pet** Potok, Gova.   a   b

2. I **pet** my Potok, Gova.   a   b

 The underlined words in these sentences from the story have more than one meaning. The meanings are written in the box. On each blank, write the letter of the meaning of the word that fits in that sentence.

3 _____ I <u>ran</u> my hand over Gova's soft, orange feathers.

4. _____ His words stopped me <u>cold</u>.

5. _____ When the rulers found out, they <u>broke</u> up the Pod.

6. _____ I'll be <u>back</u> as soon as I can.

ran	**a.**	moved quickly using legs, faster than walking
	b.	moved easily across
cold	**a.**	quickly or with shock
	b.	not warm
broke	**a.**	without money
	b.	split or separated
back	**a.**	the rear part of the body
	b.	at the starting place

79

Name _____ Date _____

Strategy: Making Inferences, Drawing Conclusions

When you make inferences or draw conclusions, you figure out information that is not written in the story you are reading. You do this by using details and your own experiences. Sometimes stories tell about how a person looks, thinks, feels, or talks. Ask yourself whether this person is like other people you know. Think about how you would act or feel in that person's place. Thinking about yourself and others will help you draw conclusions about the people in the stories you read.

 Read the passage below. Then make an inference or draw a conclusion about why Martin Luther King, Jr., did what he did.

> Martin Luther King, Jr., worked for equal rights. People of all **races** paid the same **fare** for the bus. The law said that African Americans had to sit in the back of the bus. Martin Luther King, Jr., thought the law was unfair.
>
> He spoke out for the **civil rights** movement. He risked being **fined** or going to **prison** if he was found **guilty** of breaking the law. Once he was led to jail in **handcuffs**. He had to see a **lawyer**. Martin Luther King, Jr., kept working for **constitutional** rights, though. He helped make life better for U.S. **minorities**.

 Why did Martin Luther King, Jr., work so hard for equal rights? Write what you think. Then tell what details in the passage made you draw this conclusion.

I think Martin Luther King, Jr., did this because _____

_____.

These details from the passage made me
think this.

1. _____

2. _____

> **Thinking about more than just what a passage says will make what you read more interesting.**

Name _____ Date _____

Vocabulary Builder

The words in the box come from the passage you just read. You will see these words again in the selection you are about to read.

 Complete the puzzle below. This will help you remember each word and its meaning. The first word has been done for you.

fare
~~races~~
constitutional
handcuffs
prison
lawyer
civil rights
guilty
fined
minorities

Across

2. Groups of people with similar skin and hair color could be called _____.
6. _____ rights are rights allowed by a country's laws.
8. If you pay money to ride a bus, train, or taxi, you are paying a _____.
9. If you have done something wrong, then you are _____.
10. This is another word for jail.

Down

1. These are metal rings used to hold someone's hands together.
3. These are the rights of every citizen.
4. Groups that are different from the largest group are _____.
5. If someone is made to pay money for doing something wrong, he or she is _____.
7. A person who practices law for a living is a _____.

Purpose for Reading

Now you are going to read a passage about Claudette Colvin. She was a young person who helped change the lives of many African Americans. While you read, think about what it would have been like to be her.

Claudette Breaks the Law

On March 2, 1955, a city bus rolled along the streets of Montgomery, Alabama. Some of its riders were going to work. Others were going shopping or going home. The bus stopped at different street corners. Some people got on the bus, while others stepped off.

There was a difference between the people leaving the bus through the front door and those leaving through the back door. The difference was the color of their skin. White people could leave the bus through the front door. African Americans were allowed to exit only through the back door.

1. How do you think African American people felt about having to use the back door of the bus?

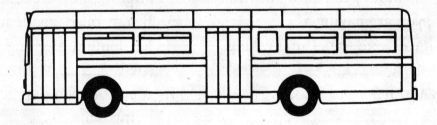

There were other rules African Americans had to follow on city buses. It was against the law for them to sit across from white people or in front of whites. If there weren't enough seats, African Americans had to give their seats to whites.

At one stop, 15-year-old Claudette Colvin climbed onto the bus with her books. She paid her **fare**. Then she got off the bus so that she could enter through the back door with other African Americans. There were no white riders on the bus. Claudette sat down near the middle. She finished eating her candy bar.

The bus filled with riders, both white and African American. The driver looked back and saw that Claudette had not given her seat to a white passenger. He called to her to get up, but she stayed in the seat. A white woman sat across from Claudette and frowned. Claudette did not move, even though it was against the law to stay where she was.

"Hey, get up!" the white bus driver shouted. Claudette still refused to move. Other people on the bus began to complain.

Angrily, the driver jumped up. He said he was going to call the police.

Claudette did not move. She believed the law that separated people on buses was wrong. People of different **races** should be able to sit together.

> **2. Do you think Claudette was brave to sit where she wanted to sit? Tell why you think that.**

---

fare (FEHR) *noun* A fare is money paid to ride a bus, train, or taxi.
races (RAYS uhz) *noun* Races are groups of people. People in each group share the same beginnings from long ago. They usually have similar eye and skin color.

The bus driver called to a traffic officer. The officer came onto the bus and asked Claudette if she would get up.

Claudette said, "I paid my fare, so I do not have to get up. It's my **constitutional** right!"

Taken Away

The bus driver called for more police to get Claudette off the bus. She held her books tightly. She told the police that they had no right to make her give up her seat.

The police knocked Claudette's books down. They lifted and carried her off the bus. She kicked and screamed.

The officers put Claudette into a police car. They put **handcuffs** on her. Then they drove her to the Montgomery City Hall.

City Hall was the government center of Montgomery. The men took Claudette inside the building. One man who saw her said, "Take her to Atmore, and get rid of her." Atmore was the state **prison**.

While Claudette was in City Hall, other students who had been with her on the bus went home. They told Claudette's mother what had happened.

Claudette's mother called a **lawyer** named Fred Gray. He worked on **civil rights** cases. Civil rights are rights that the U.S. Constitution gives everyone in the country.

With Fred Gray beside her, Claudette told the judge she was not **guilty** of breaking the law. The judge said she was guilty. He **fined** her and sent her home.

---

constitutional (kahn stuh TOO shuh nuhl) *adjective* Constitutional means "allowed by a country's system of laws."

handcuffs (HAND kuhfs) *noun* Handcuffs are metal rings that hold someone's hands together.

prison (PRIHZ uhn) *noun* A prison is a jail, or a place where people are kept for doing something that is against the law.

lawyer (LAW yuhr) *noun* A lawyer is someone who practices law for a living.

civil rights (SIHV uhl RYTS) *adjective* Civil rights means "having to do with rights that belong to every citizen."

guilty (GIHL tee) *adjective* Guilty means "having done something wrong."

fined (FYND) *verb* Fined means "made someone pay money for doing something wrong."

---

3. Why do you think Claudette said she was not guilty?

Home Again

Claudette found her life changed after her experience. Some people in her neighborhood did not understand why she had done what she'd done. Some students at school stayed away from her.

Claudette knew her neighbors and friends wanted change. They just did not know how to go about it.

There were others who agreed with Claudette's actions. Many were members of the NAACP, the National Association for the Advancement of Colored People. This group worked to change bad laws for **minorities**. Fred Gray was a member. Claudette joined the NAACP youth group.

---

minorities (my NAWR uh teez) *noun* Minorities are small groups of people who are different in some ways from a larger group.

How could someone be treated so unfairly in the United States? The United States was a country that said all people were equal. But Claudette was an African American. To some people, that meant she did not have to be treated the same as other people.

4. Do you think Claudette was angry about what happened to her? Tell why you think that.

Thinking About the Selection

 Fill in the circle of the correct answer.

① This passage is mostly about—

Ⓐ the history of slavery in the United States.

Ⓑ the people who fought for the civil rights cause.

Ⓒ what one person did to help the civil rights cause.

Ⓓ how the U.S. government works.

② What word best describes Claudette Colvin?

Ⓐ old   Ⓒ shy

Ⓑ brave   Ⓓ frightened

③ The judge said Claudette was guilty because she—

Ⓐ rode the bus without paying.   Ⓒ fought with the police.

Ⓑ got off at the front of the bus.   Ⓓ went against the rules.

④ Why was Claudette treated differently than some of the other people on the bus?

Ⓐ She was African American.

Ⓑ She was young.

Ⓒ She rode the bus without paying.

Ⓓ She spoke another language.

⑤ Why did Claudette Colvin refuse to get up from her seat on the bus?

_____

_____

⑥ Claudette said she was not guilty. Explain why she said this.

_____

_____

Name _____   Date _____

Prewriting

Idea Web

In "Claudette Breaks the Law," Claudette Colvin fought against a law that she thought was wrong. Her actions helped change the law. Think about a law or rule that you think should be changed. Why would you change it?

 Fill in the web below. Tell what law or rule you think is wrong. Then tell three reasons why it should be changed.

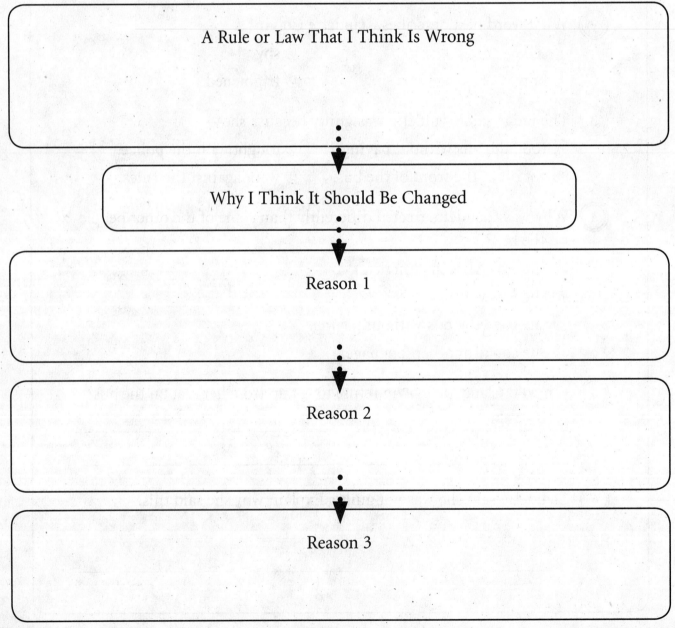

A Rule or Law That I Think Is Wrong

Why I Think It Should Be Changed

Reason 1

Reason 2

Reason 3

88

A Plan for Writing

Writing to Persuade

A persuasive essay tells an opinion. The writer tries to get people to think or feel the same way he or she does. The writer must offer good reasons, or people might not change their minds.

 Write a persuasive essay to tell about a rule or law that should be changed. Make people realize why it should be changed. Use ideas from your web.

Tell what is wrong.

A rule or law that should be changed is _____

_____.

Explain your first reason.

There are three reasons why it should be changed.

This *rule / law* (circle one) should be changed because ____

_____

_____.

Explain your second reason.

It should also be changed because _____

_____.

Explain your last reason.

The last reason this *rule / law* (circle one) should be

changed is _____

_____.

Writing

 Write a persuasive essay to tell about a rule or law that you think should be changed. Use the plan above to help you. Tell why you think the rule or law is wrong. Tell why it should be changed. You can give more details, but go in the same order as your plan. Write your essay on a separate sheet of paper.

Name _____ Date _____

Breaking the Code

Sounds of *ou*

The letters *ou* can stand for many different sounds. You can hear these different sounds in *soup, cough, couple, four,* and *mouse.*

soup

cough

couple

four

mouse

 Read the words with the sounds of *ou* in the list. Fill in the blanks to complete each sentence with one or more words.

young about South would you thought

1. The races were not _____ of as equal in the _____.

2. African Americans wanted change but didn't know how to go

_____ it.

3. Claudette Colvin was a _____ person who made a difference.

4. Do _____ think you _____ have done what she did?

 Choose a word from the box. Write it on the blank beside the word that shares the same sound of *ou*.

bought group your could shout double

5. house _____

6. should _____

7. youth _____

8. pour _____

9. trouble _____

10. brought _____

Words, Words, Words

Using Reference Materials

Reference materials are books you use to learn something. If you want to learn what a word means, you look in the dictionary.

The words listed in a dictionary are called *entry words*. These words are in alphabetical order. The dictionary tells the meaning of these words. If a word has more than one meaning, each one is numbered.

To find the page that has the word you are looking for, look at the top of the page. The words at the top of the page are called *guide words*. These words show you the first and last word on that page.

 Read the dictionary entry below. Then answer the questions.

---

race 1. *noun* a contest of speed 2. *verb* to run 3. *noun* a group of people who are alike in some way, such as skin, eye, or hair color

---

1. Circle the two guide words that might appear at the top of the page listing the word *race*. What two words would *race* come between?

   rack and radio   radio and rain

   raccoon and radar   rabbit and raccoon

2. How many meanings are given for the word *race*? _____

3. Circle the number of the meaning that is used in this sentence:

   I ran quickly in the race.   1   2   3

4. Now write your own sentence using the word *race*.

Name _____ Date _____

Strategy: Recognizing Author's Viewpoint, Purpose

Authors have their own reasons for writing stories or passages. An author's reason for writing is called the *author's purpose*. When you read, you should try to understand how authors think and why they write. This will help you think more carefully about what you read.

 Read the passage below. Think about the author's viewpoint and purpose.

> If you are a **teenager** who wants to be a **baby-sitter**, anything can happen. You can be **assured** things will not go as you plan.
>
> Bits of **cereal** can end up on the floor instead of in the baby's mouth. The baby might find **amusement** in pulling books off a **bookcase**. Books you **eased** back on the shelves might come off again. The baby might hit her head on a **doorknob**.
>
> Don't let this **annoy** you! If you are careful, you can live up to your **potential** as a baby-sitter.

 Check ✔ the box next to the choice that you think best describes the author's purpose for writing this passage. On the next two lines, describe what made you think this was the author's purpose.

> **Thinking about the author's purpose will help you understand and remember what you read.**

The author's purpose for writing was to—

☐ explain what you should do as a baby-sitter.

☐ give you a tip that might help you be a better baby-sitter.

☐ make you laugh by telling a funny story.

I think this was the author's purpose for writing because _____

_____.

An author might have more than one reason for writing. This author wanted to help baby-sitters be more careful and also probably wanted to write in a funny way.

Name _____ Date _____

Vocabulary Builder

The words in the box come from the passage you just read. You will see these words again in the story you are about to read.

 Complete each sentence with one of the words. The first one has been done for you.

teenager
cereal
amusement
eased
potential
~~*doorknob*~~
assured
annoy
baby-sitter
bookcase

1. I am the word ____*doorknob*____. I am the handle on a door.

2. I am the word _____. I will take care of children for you.

3. I am the word _____. I am not old, and I am not young. I become me at age 13.

4. I am the word _____. I am made of wheat, rice, oats, or corn. You might have had me for breakfast.

5. I am the word _____. I am entertainment or fun.

6. I am the word _____. I am a set of shelves for books.

7. I am the word _____. Other words for me are *irritate*, *disturb*, or *displease*.

8. I am the word _____. If you moved carefully, that was me.

9. I am the word _____. With me, you are certain. The word *sure* is in me.

10. I am the word _____. If you do all that you can, then you live up to me.

Purpose for Reading

Now you are going to read a story. Koby thinks he is going to have a fun summer, but he didn't plan on writing book reports. Read to find out what happens in Koby's "Party Summer."

www.harcourtschoolsupply.com
93
Unit 2: Ten-Book Summer
Reading Workout Book 2, SV 9781419099052

Party Summer

This was it, day one of Party Summer. It was my first summer as a **teenager**. School was out, and I was 13. Things were going to be different.

This wasn't going to be a little-kid summer of hanging around the apartment. This summer was going to be hot sun, cold water, and teenaged girls. My best friend, Bud, and I planned to hang out at the Sun Fun Pool every day.

I finished my **cereal** as quickly as I could. The sooner we got to the pool, the sooner the **amusement** could begin.

---

1. What kind of story do you think the author is going to tell? Explain why you think so.

"Korbett!" Dad yelled from the living room. "We need to talk."

That was a bad sign. Everyone calls me Koby. Nobody calls me Korbett unless I'm in trouble.

Dad came into the kitchen. "Your mom and I are upset about your grades," he said.

It was summer. Why worry about grades now?

"Everybody's grades dropped last year," I said. "Middle school is hard."

---

teenager (TEEN ay juhr) *noun* A teenager is someone who is between 13 and 19 years old.
cereal (SIHR ee uhl) *noun* Cereal is a breakfast food eaten with milk.
amusement (uh MYOOZ muhnt) *noun* An amusement is something that is fun to do.

"How many times have I told you that grades are important?" he asked.

He'd told me a million times, and I didn't want to hear it again.

"You're right, Dad," I said. "I'll try harder." I **eased** toward the door.

"Not so fast, son," he said. "Your teacher says that you don't work up to your **potential**. That means you can do the work, but you don't. You're lazy."

> **2. Do you think the author believes that school is important? Tell why you think that.**

---

eased (EEZD) *verb* Someone who has eased has moved slowly and carefully.

potential (poh TEHN shuhl) *noun* Someone's potential is the high level that they are able to meet but haven't reached yet.

"OK," I said. "But could we talk about this later? Bud's expecting me."

Dad glared. "I'll come right to the point. Your mother thinks you should read five books as a summer project."

"Five books!" I howled.

"But now I think that isn't such a good idea," he added.

"Whew! Thanks, Dad." I grabbed the **doorknob**.

He raised his voice to stop me. "I think ten books would be better."

"No fair!" I cried.

"And I want a written report on each," he said.

"Nobody does book reports in the summer," I complained.

"You will. Ten of them," Dad **assured** me. He walked off without another word.

Ten books were more than I had read in my whole life. The thought of all those words worried me, but I couldn't let this get me down. I'd just have to figure a way out of it later.

---

3. How do you think Koby is going to get out of doing his book reports?

Rushing out the apartment door, I ran right into my neighbor, Nina Song. Nina is my age and has had a crush on me forever.

---

doorknob (DAWR nahb) *noun* A doorknob is a handle used to open a door.
assured (uh SHURD) *verb* Assured means "made someone sure of something."

"What are you doing here?" I asked. "I thought you were spending the summer with your mom in Miami."

"No," she said. "Dad wants me to stay with him."

Right. I think she wanted to stay here just to **annoy** me.

"Where are we going?" she asked, falling into step beside me.

"WE aren't going anywhere," I corrected her. "I'M going to Bud's. And I'm late!"

I ran for the stairs. I know it was mean of me. Nina couldn't keep up with me there.

annoy (uh NOY) *verb* To annoy someone is to bother that person.

In five minutes I was at Bud's door two floors down.

"Hurry!" I said. "Let's get to the pool before something else goes wrong."

"I can't go, man." Bud calls everyone *man*.

"But we have plans," I reminded him.

"So does my mom," he answered. "Her plans are for me to stay home with my little sister."

"You're spoiling Party Summer," I whined.

Bud shrugged. "I can't help it, man. Mom says she's not paying a **baby-sitter** to watch Katy when I can do it. Mothers can be such pains."

"Fathers, too," I said. I told him about my dad's ten-book plan.

"Oh, that's not so bad. Book reports are easy," Bud said. "All you have to do is copy that stuff from the back of the book."

Bud looked in his desk, on a **bookcase** or two, and finally under his bed. He found one of his old reports and gave it to me.

"Thanks," I said. I stuck the paper into my pocket. At least one of my problems was solved.

---

4. Do you think Koby's problem is solved? Tell why you think that.

---

baby-sitter (BAY bee siht uhr) *noun* A baby-sitter is someone who is paid to watch children whose parents aren't home.

bookcase (BUK kays) *noun* A bookcase is furniture for holding books.

Thinking About the Selection

 Fill in the circle of the correct answer.

1. This story is mostly about—
   Ⓐ all the fun that Koby has during the summer.
   Ⓑ how Koby's summer is not turning out as planned.
   Ⓒ how to check out books at the library.
   Ⓓ Koby's friends, Bud and Nina.

2. Why is Koby looking forward to the summer?
   Ⓐ He plans to spend time reading more books.
   Ⓑ He wants to spend time with his girlfriend, Nina.
   Ⓒ He is going to Miami to stay with his mother.
   Ⓓ He thinks he will go to the pool with Bud and meet girls.

3. Why do Koby's parents ask him to write the reports?
   Ⓐ They want him to get ahead for school next year.
   Ⓑ He has to do them for summer school.
   Ⓒ They are worried about his grades in school.
   Ⓓ They want him to have something fun to do with Bud.

4. You could guess that after this Koby will—
   Ⓐ go to the library with Bud.
   Ⓑ plan to stay home to read.
   Ⓒ try to find a way out of reading books.
   Ⓓ start a book club with Bud and Nina.

5. What details does the author tell the reader to help describe Koby?

   _____

   _____

6. Will Bud's plan solve Koby's problem? Tell why you think it will or will not.

   _____

   _____

Name _____ Date _____

Idea Chart

In "Party Summer," Koby tries to get out of reading. He probably can't write the reports by copying book covers. He'll have to read the books. Think about a book you have read. Would you tell Koby to read this book? Why or why not?

 Fill in the chart below. Give two reasons why you like the book and two reasons why you do not like it. Then tell whether you would suggest that others read it.

The title of the book: _____

The author of the book: _____

The book is about: _____

What I Like About the Book	**What I Don't Like About the Book**
1. _____	1. _____
_____	_____
_____	_____
2. _____	2. _____
_____	_____
_____	_____

Would I tell someone to read this book?   yes / no

A Plan for Writing

Book Review

A review tells people what is good and bad about something. It often helps people decide if something is worth their time or money.

 Write a review of a book you have read. Explain if you think someone else would like it. Use ideas from your chart.

Describe what you are reviewing.

Tell what you like about the book.

Tell what you don't like about the book.

Tell if someone else should read it.

This is a review of _____ by _____.

It is about _____.

I like this book because _____

_____.

Also, _____.

I don't like this book because _____

_____.

Also, _____.

I think that most people *would / would not* (circle one) like this book. I suggest that other people *should / should not*

(circle one) read it because _____

_____

Writing

 Write a book review. Use the plan above to help you. Describe what you like and what you do not like about the book. Then tell whether you think others should read it. You can use more details, but follow the order of your plan. Write your review on a separate sheet of paper.

Name _____ Date _____

Breaking the Code

Sound of *oi* and *oy*

The letters *oi* and *oy* can stand for the vowel sound you hear in the words *coin* and *toy*. The letters *oi* are often found in the middle of a word. The letters *oy* are often, but not always, found at the end of a word.

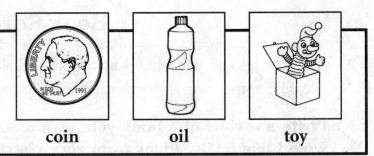

coin   oil   toy

➡️ **Circle the word with the *oi/oy* sound that fits in each sentence. Then write the word in the blank.**

1. Koby wants to _____ this summer.

   enjoy   boil   point

2. Koby might be _____ this summer.

   royal   disappointed   joined

3. The book reports might _____ it.

   oil   join   spoil

4. Koby says that Nina is _____ to him.

   loyal   annoying   noise

➡️ **Fill in the blanks with the letters *oi* or *oy* to complete each word.**

5. Koby is a b _____ _____ .

6. He is trying to av _____ _____ d reading books.

7. Doesn't he know there is j _____ _____ in reading a good book?

8. Will he make the right ch _____ _____ ce?

Words, Words, Words

Compound Words

Compound words are made of two smaller words. There were many compound words in the story you read. For example, the word *doorknob* is made of two smaller words.

door + knob = doorknob

These smaller words help you know the meaning of the compound word. Look at the words *door* and *knob*. They show that a doorknob is the knob that helps you open a door.

 Read the words in the boxes. Then read the sentences below. Choose one word from box A and one word from box B to make a compound word that fits in each sentence. Each word is used once.

A	
for	teen
girl	any
some	no

B	
aged	ever
where	friend
body	thing

1. My name is Koby, and _____ calls me Korbett unless I am in trouble.

2. This summer was going to be about hot sun, cold water, and _____ girls.

3. Nina has had a crush on me _____.

4. Nina is not my _____.

5. Nina and I aren't going _____.

6. Bud and I need to get to the pool before _____ else goes wrong.

Name _____ Date _____

Strategy: Recognizing Author's Viewpoint, Purpose

Authors have different viewpoints, or ideas, about what they choose to write. They also have different purposes, or reasons, for writing. If an author wants to teach the reader how to do something, then the author probably thinks this thing is important. If an author writes to get the reader to think a different way about something, this is probably the way the author thinks.

 Read the passage below. Think about the author's viewpoint.

> How important are school sports? This is a good **debate** topic. Athletes are sometimes treated differently. Some people might think these differences are unfair. Their **point of view** should be heard.
>
> My school **principal** had a **persuasive argument**. She said other **cultures** might disagree, but sports are important here. She thinks schools should help athletes.
>
> I asked for **elaboration**. She said her job is to help students from all **backgrounds** do well in everything. Her **advice** is that schools should help all students in all activities. I agree with her **opinion**.

 Check ✓ the box next to the choice that you think best describes this author's viewpoint. Then describe what made you think this was the author's viewpoint.

The author's viewpoint on sports is that—

☐ sports are more important than other activities.

☐ sports, classes, and other activities are all important.

☐ classes are more important than activities outside of class.

I think this is the author's viewpoint because _____

_____ .

Remember that sometimes you have to guess what the author thinks. Use what the author chooses to write about and the words the author uses as clues.

Thinking about the author's viewpoint will help you be a more thoughtful reader.

Name _____ Date _____

Vocabulary Builder

The words in the box come from the passage you just read. You will see these words again in the story you are about to read.

➡ **Choose a word from the box to complete each sentence. Write the letters of the word on the blanks. The first word has been done for you. When you are finished, the letters in the circles will tell how the teacher you will read about feels.**

| debate |
| persuasive |
| point of view |
| backgrounds |
| cultures |
| ~~principal~~ |
| argument |
| elaboration |
| opinion |
| advice |

① The person who heads a school is a (p) r i n c i p a l.

② Large groups of people with certain ways of doing things are _ _ _ _ _O_ _ .

③ When an author tells how he feels about something, he is telling his _O_ _ _ _ _ _ _ _ _ _ .

④ People who don't agree might have an _ _ _O_ _ _ _ .

⑤ People from different _ _ _ _ _ _ _ _ _O_ can be friends.

⑥ If a sentence is not a fact, it might be an _ _ _ _O_ _ .

⑦ To make a good decision, get _O_ _ _ _ from someone you trust.

⑧ O_ _ _ _ _ _ _ _ _ _ , or using details, is important in writing.

⑨ _ _ _O_ _ concerns a discussion of both sides of an argument.

⑩ A person who can change people's minds is very _ _ _O_ _ _ _ _ .

Answer: She is _ _ _ _ _ to teach _ _ _ _ _ _ .

Purpose for Reading

Now you are going to read about the opinions of a teacher named Ms. T. Read on to find out what this teacher says about her students.

My Students

Ms. T.

I teach high school **debate**, public speaking, and English III. In all three classes, students learn the art of **persuasive** speaking and writing. When someone speaks or writes in a persuasive way, that person gives reasons to get the listener or reader to take the same **point of view**. Persuasive writing and speaking can be very strong. It is important that students use these tools for what they believe is right.

Most of my students have strong feelings about what is right. They are a great group, and I love to watch them work together.

They come from many **backgrounds**. Some students are from other countries with **cultures** very different from our own. Other students are the first people in their families to be born in this country. Still others are from families who have lived in our country for many years. One can easily see that their interests are also very different. My students are artists, class clowns, "straight A" students, and class leaders, to name a few.

---

debate (dee BAYT) *noun* A debate is a talk in which people share different points or different ideas about something.

persuasive (puhr SWAY sihv) *adjective* To be persuasive is to try to change someone's mind about something.

point of view (POYNT UHV VYOO) *noun* A point of view is a way of looking at things.

backgrounds (BAK growndz) *noun* Backgrounds are people's experiences and history.

cultures (KUHL chuhrz) *noun* Cultures are large groups of people, often whole countries, that have certain ways of doing things.

Because of all their differences, it is wonderful to watch these students exchange ideas. This is where their sense of what is right really shows. They don't point out one another's differences. Instead my students use their differences to get new views and fresh ideas.

1. What do you think the author means by "their sense of what is right"?

Reading Workout Book 2, SV 9781419099052

As you can guess, all these differences can lead to quite a few exciting talks! My students often come to class before the bell rings. Someone might read a newspaper story to the class. Another student might say something about the morning message from the **principal**. That's all it takes to get this bunch going. They will talk about almost anything. Every one of them seems to love putting his or her persuasive-speaking skills to the test.

2. Why do you think these students like to try to persuade others to agree with them?

Classroom visitors might think my students are having an **argument**. They are really using what they know and how they feel to carefully put together a persuasive argument. This type of argument is not the same as an argument you have because you are angry. That kind of argument is often based on feelings.

A persuasive argument is based on **elaboration**. Students carefully build details to prove their point of view. The students work on building their argument. They add more and more details—stories and facts—to get their fellow students to agree with their **opinion**. If you knew this group like I know them, you would realize one thing. They will try their hardest not to give in to anyone else's point of view!

---

principal (PRIHN suh puhl) *noun* A principal is a person who leads a school.

argument (AHR gyoo muhnt) *noun* An argument is a talk in which a person is trying to get someone else to see something in a different way.

elaboration (ee lab uh RAY shuhn) *noun* Elaboration is the use of many details to tell about something.

opinion (uh PIHN yuhn) *noun* An opinion is how someone feels or what he or she believes about something.

---

3. Which do you think would help make a more persuasive argument, facts or feelings? Tell why you think so.

Beginning debate students often tell me that they can't speak in a persuasive way. There is no possible way that they can get up in front of the class to give a persuasive speech. When I ask them why not, they rattle off a long list of reasons, such as:

"Oh, Miss, I get too upset, and it keeps me from speaking in front of people."

"Some wise people say you learn more by watching rather than speaking, so I'm just following the great masters' **advice**."

These students don't realize that they have just made use of persuasive speaking. Without even thinking about it, they have built an argument. They have stated why they should be excused from doing class work!

---

advice (ad VYS) *noun* Advice is something a person tells someone in order to help him or her decide something.

My students are well on their way to becoming very good speakers and writers. Their skills in persuasive speaking and writing and their ideas of what is fair and right will take them far in life. I greatly admire these students, and I am proud to share my time with them.

4. How do you think these students' skills will take them far in life?

Name _____ Date _____

 Fill in the circle of the correct answer.

1 Ms. T. says that the best way to build a persuasive argument is to—
Ⓐ discuss how one feels.
Ⓑ talk to people who feel the same.
Ⓒ use details, stories, and facts.
Ⓓ speak with strong feeling.

2 Because her students come from many different backgrounds, Ms. T. says that they—
Ⓐ have exciting exchanges of ideas.
Ⓑ cannot get along well together.
Ⓒ do not know how to talk to each other.
Ⓓ are not happy to be in class together

3 How does Ms. T. feel about her job?
Ⓐ bored   Ⓒ tired
Ⓑ proud   Ⓓ upset

4 Ms. T. probably wrote this passage to—
Ⓐ tell readers about the importance of sharing different beliefs.
Ⓑ delight readers with funny stories about a high school.
Ⓒ teach readers to be better speakers, readers, and writers.
Ⓓ ask readers to become teachers.

5 What is the difference between arguing when you are angry and making a persuasive argument?

_____

_____

6 Give two reasons Ms. T. enjoys working with her students.

_____

_____

WRITE ABOUT IT!

Name ______________________________ Date ____________________

Prewriting

Graphic Organizer

In "My Students," Ms. T. tells about her students' strong beliefs. She also tells how her students' ideas are different. Think about two people you respect for doing what is right. They could be famous people or people you know. How are they alike? How are they different?

➔ **Fill in the circles below. In one circle, tell about one person you respect. In the other, tell about another person you respect. In each circle, tell how that person is different from the other. In the middle where the circles meet, tell how these people are alike.**

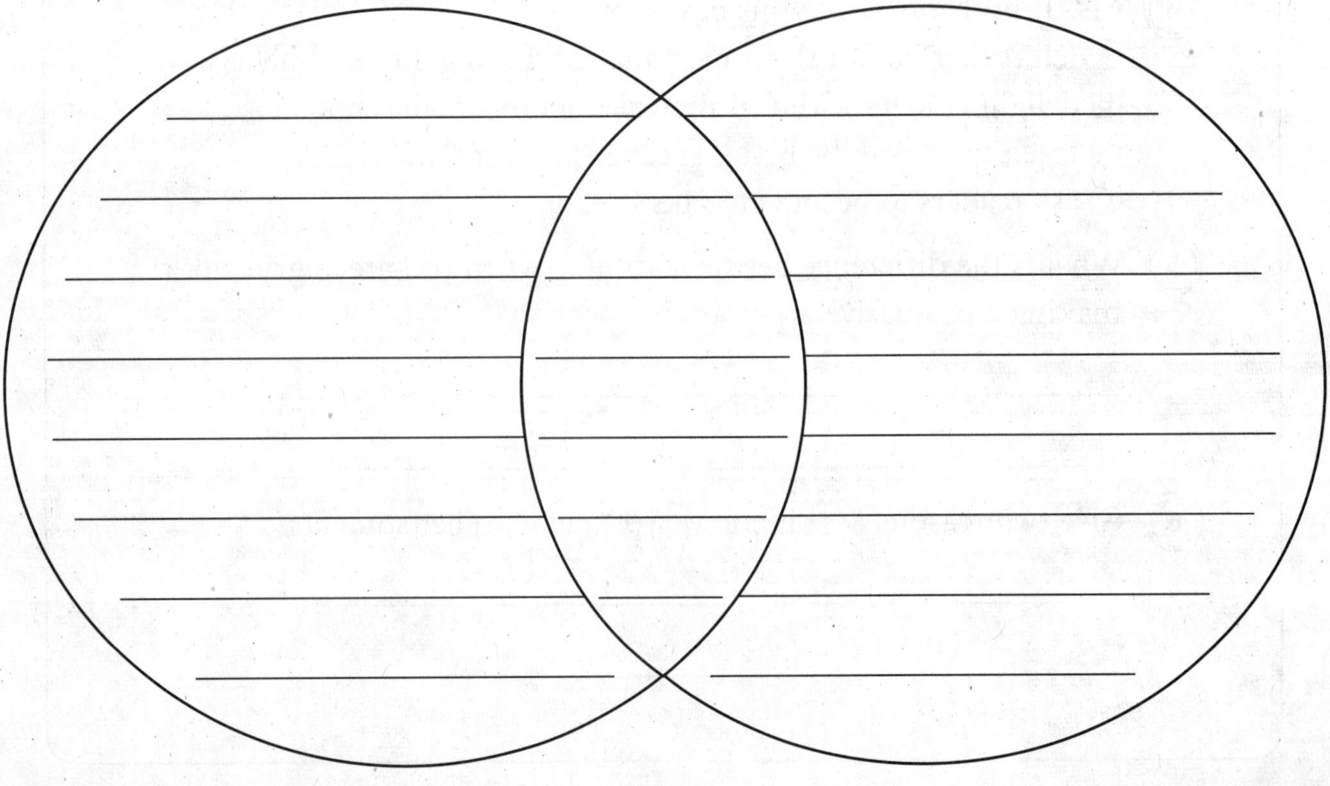

I respect: ______________________

Why I respect this person: ____________

____

____

I respect: ______________________

Why I respect this person: ____________

____

____

Reading Workout Book 2, SV 9781419099052

Name _____   Date _____

A Plan for Writing

Writing to Compare and Contrast

An essay gives information and ideas. An essay must have details to support the main idea. Sometimes an essay tells how two things are alike and different.

 Write an essay to compare and contrast two people you respect. Tell who these people are and how they are alike and different. Also tell why you respect them both. Use ideas from your diagram.

Tell who you respect.

Explain their differences.

Explain how they are alike.

Two people I respect are _____ and _____.

These people are different in some ways, but they are also alike.

One way that these two people are different is _____

_____.

They are also different because _____

_____.

These people are alike in some ways. One way they are

alike is that _____.

They are also alike because _____

I respect both of these people. I respect them because

_____.

Writing

 Write an essay to compare and contrast two people you respect. Use the plan above to help you. Tell how the people are alike and different. Also tell why you respect them. You can give more details, but go in the same order as your plan. Write your essay on a separate sheet of paper.

Name _____ Date _____

Breaking the Code

Silent Letters *k*, *w*, and *gh*

Sometimes letters are silent. The *k* in **knot**, the *w* in **wrist**, and the *gh* in **light** are all silent. This means that when you read these words out loud, you do not hear the sounds of these letters.

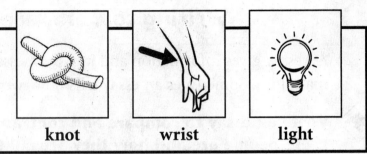

knot   wrist   light

 Circle the word with the silent letters *k*, *w*, or *gh* that fits best in each sentence. Then write the word in the blank.

1. Ms. T. gave her _____ about teaching.
   thoughts   speech   worries

2. Ms. T. teaches speaking and _____.
   knitting   debating   writing

3. She teaches in a _____ school.
   high   tough   wrong

4. She enjoys sharing her _____ with students.
   speeches   knowledge   sight

 Complete each sentence with a word from the box. Then circle the silent letter or letters in the word.

fight	wrong
right	know

5. Ms. T. says you should argue for what you think is _____.

6. In a debate, you should _____ a lot about your subject.

7. If you disagree with someone, you might think that person is _____.

8. Ms. T. would say you should argue but not _____.

Unit 2: Tough Choices
Reading Workout Book 2, SV 9781419099052

Name_____   Date_____

Words, Words, Words

Prefixes

A prefix is a set of letters that can be added to the beginning of some words. A prefix changes the word's meaning. The word *prefix* even has a prefix—the letters *pre*. This prefix is also in the word *preschool*. From reading the words *prefix* and *preschool*, you can probably guess that *pre* means "before."

 Read the sentences in the box. See how the meaning of the underlined word changes when a prefix is added.

Before I started <u>school</u>, I went to preschool.

Last year I got a <u>new</u> library card. This year I have to renew it.

 The words in the box can complete the sentences below, but each needs the prefix *re* added. The prefix *re* means "back" or "again." Add *re* to each word and write each new word on the correct line.

write	turned	cycle	view

1. When I am not happy with an essay, I ask my teacher if I can

_____ it.

2. Before a test, you should _____ your notes so you do not forget anything.

3. I believe that we should _____ the paper we use in school.

4. We were happy when Ms. T. _____ to class after being gone a week.

Do the Right Thing—Wrap-Up

The Silver Ring

Tara pulled off her gym clothes and reached into her gym bag. After searching for a moment, she started tossing books on the floor.

"What are you doing?" asked her best friend, Emma.

"Looking for my new silver ring with the heart charm," Tara said. "I got it for my birthday, and it's gone!"

"Are you sure you put it in your gym bag?" Emma asked.

"Yes, I'm sure. Now I can't find it!"

"Do you think someone stole it?"

Tara nodded.

1. What caused Tara to think her ring had been stolen?

"You'd better tell Mrs. Sutton."

The two girls walked to the teacher's office and tapped on the door. "Yes?" called Mrs. Sutton.

"I think someone stole my ring while we were on the track, Mrs. Sutton. It was in the bottom of my . . . ." Tara's voice failed as the teacher shook her head.

"What have I told you girls about rings and necklaces?"

"Give them to you to lock in your office," Tara whispered.

116

"If you don't follow the rules, what can you expect?" Mrs. Sutton asked.

Tara and Emma looked at each other and walked away. They joined their friends in the lunchroom. Suddenly Tara grabbed Emma's arm. "Look over there! Jill's wearing my ring!"

"How can you tell?" Emma whispered.

"Because it's just like mine. How would she get a ring like that? I'm going to get it back."

2. What do you think Tara will do about the ring?

Tara pushed her chair back from the table and charged toward Jill. "You thief!" she shouted. "How dare you take my ring?"

Jill's face turned red. She jumped from her chair and ran toward the nearest door.

Tara turned to Emma. "I'm going to tell the principal."

Ten minutes later, the principal sent the girls to their next class. He promised to do what he could.

English class seemed to last forever. Tara stared at her silver ring on Jill's hand. After a while, an office helper entered the room and handed a hall pass to the teacher.

"Jill," Miss Flores called. "You're wanted in the office."

Jill followed the office helper out the door. When she came back, she handed Miss Flores a yellow slip of paper. As she moved toward her seat, she flashed an angry look at Tara.

Miss Flores glanced at the paper. "Tara, now you're wanted in the office." Tara rushed out the door.

"She says the ring is hers?" Tara shouted a few minutes later. "She's lying! She's a thief and a liar!"

"No, she's not lying," the principal said. "I talked to Jill's mother. She said Jill's aunt gave her the ring."

Tara didn't know what to think. She stamped out of the office and back to class. She dropped into her chair and stuck her hand into her purse for a piece of gum. Suddenly her fingers touched a small, cold object. She felt the object with the tips of her fingers. Without looking, she knew it was her ring.

---

3. How do you think Tara felt when she found the ring in her purse?

Tara closed her eyes. She pushed the ring back to the bottom of her purse. She couldn't let anyone see it, not after she had called Jill a thief.

For the rest of the day, Tara worried about her problem.

The next day at lunch, Tara walked across the lunchroom. She didn't look at her friends. Instead, she went straight to Jill. "Can I talk to you for a minute?" Tara asked.

"Why? So you can call me more names? No, thanks." Jill pushed her chair back from the table.

"No, please wait. I need to tell you something."

"Leave me alone. I didn't take your ring."

Tara swallowed a lump in her throat. "I know you didn't take it. I found it later in my purse. I thought it had been stolen. When I walked into the lunchroom, I saw you wearing a ring like mine. You had never worn that ring before, so I just . . . ."

"You never look at me. How would you know what I wear?" interrupted Jill.

"Look, I know I was wrong. I shouldn't have said what I did. I'm really sorry."

"Now everybody in the whole school thinks I'm a thief." Jill's voice shook.

"I know. I need to fix that," Tara agreed. "I'm so sorry."

Jill didn't say a word. She rose from her chair and headed toward the door. As soon as Jill left the room, Emma rushed over to Tara. "What was that about?" she asked. "Did you get your ring back?"

"Jill didn't take my ring," Tara mumbled.

"What? But she was wearing it!"

Tara's face turned bright red. "No, the ring she has is hers. I found mine in my purse. I put it there instead of in my gym bag."

Emma stared at her friend. "Tara, you called her a thief! What are you going to do?"

"I told her I was sorry, but she walked away. She knows people still think she's a thief."

"So how are you going to let everyone know she's not?"

"I don't know." Tara said. She looked at Emma. "Maybe you could tell a few of our friends what happened. They could tell a few more people." She stopped as she noticed Emma's face. "No, that's not fair. I have to get out of this one by myself."

Tara sat for a minute. Then she took a deep breath and got up. She walked toward her friends and started to talk. "I need to tell you something. You see, it's like this . . . Jill didn't steal my ring. It was all a mistake."

---

4. Why do you think Tara told her friends about her mistake?

Do the Right Thing—Wrap-Up

 Fill in the circle of the correct answer.

1 This story is mostly about—
Ⓐ two good friends who do not agree about something.
Ⓑ a girl who gets a heart ring from her aunt as a present.
Ⓒ a girl who makes a mistake and then tries to fix it.
Ⓓ a girl who has her ring stolen by someone at school.

2 What was the setting for this story?
Ⓐ a school   Ⓒ a sports field
Ⓑ a house   Ⓓ a jewelry store

3 When the story says that Tara "swallowed a lump in her throat," this means she—
Ⓐ swallowed the ring.   Ⓒ felt nervous.
Ⓑ was eating her lunch.   Ⓓ was happy.

4 Jill is upset even after Tara says she found her ring because she—
Ⓐ is afraid everyone thinks she is a thief.
Ⓑ is worried Tara will find out she stole the ring.
Ⓒ thinks that she and Tara will not be friends anymore.
Ⓓ thinks she will get into more trouble with Miss Flores.

5 The author probably wrote this story in order to—
Ⓐ warn readers to check facts before blaming someone.
Ⓑ tell a story about the importance of friendship.
Ⓒ delight readers with a funny story.
Ⓓ show readers that stealing is wrong.

6 What lesson could you learn from this story? Give examples from the story to support your answer.

_____

_____

_____

Do the Right Thing—Wrap-Up

Shopping Smarts

Claudia stared at the magazine. There was an ad on the back page for a new kind of music club. If you joined the club, you got 10 brand-new CDs for 1¢! Claudia didn't like spending money for new CDs. They were so expensive at the store. Sometimes a new CD could cost as much as $18. Claudia used her money to go to the movies with her friends. She usually didn't have any left over for music.

Claudia thought about all the new CDs she wanted. The ad had a long list of CDs she could order. It said if she signed up today, she could have her new CDs in 3 weeks. Saving $180 sounded like a very good offer. Claudia decided to join the club.

1. Do you think Claudia made a good decision? Tell why you do or do not think so.

The weeks passed slowly. Claudia raced home every day to check the mail. The package finally came. Claudia was very excited. She didn't even notice the letter that came with the CDs.

Later that night, Claudia found the letter. She was shocked. The letter said she had to order 10 more CDs at the full price! There was another paper with the letter. When she opened it, Claudia was even sadder. It was a list of the CDs she had to choose from. She didn't want any of the ones on the list. Even worse, these CDs cost much more than the ones at the store. One was $24!

Claudia didn't want to buy 10 more new CDs. Now she wouldn't be able to go to the movies as often with her friends. What started out as a $180 savings ended up costing Claudia nearly $240!

---

2. Why do you think the author told you this story about Claudia?

It's a Tough World Out There

Companies make money when people buy their products. Many companies make the same kinds of products. Each company has to tell people how its product is special. Telling people about your product is called *advertising*.

Think about it. When you buy a soft drink, there are many different kinds to choose from. You probably buy the one that you think tastes the best. You might also buy one you've seen on TV. You might try a new one that you heard about from a friend. If you're trying to save money, you might just pick the cheapest one. You make your decision based on what you know about the product and what you need.

> **3. Have you ever bought something because of good advertising? Tell about this time. If you have never bought something because of advertising, tell why you buy the things you do.**

Companies use advertising to make sure that you know about their product. Sometimes they also use advertising to tell you that you need their product. Companies that use advertising often sell more products and make more money.

There are only a few rules about how to advertise. The most important one is to tell the truth. Sometimes companies try to bend the rules. Claudia's story is a good example of this kind of cheating. The music company used cheap CDs to trap Claudia. She spent more money than she planned on something she didn't really want.

Many companies use tricks like this one to get you to buy something. You have to be careful when you see ads on TV or in the newspaper. Here are some examples of tricks to watch out for.

Trick 1: If famous people like it, so will you

Suppose you see an ad for sneakers on TV. Your favorite sports star is talking about how much she likes them. You're supposed to think that if the shoes are good enough for her, then they're good enough for you. What you should know, though, is that companies pay famous people a lot of money to do these ads. The athlete is probably only saying what the company tells her to say.

Trick 2: The "free test" trap

Many companies let people test their products before buying them. The company might send out a card in the mail that offers a product for a free test. If you don't like the product, you can return it at the end of the free test period. If you forget to return the product, though, the company can charge you for it. Even if you don't want the product, you can end up with a big bill.

Trick 3: Beating the clock

Sometimes ads try to make you think you need to buy a product right away. "For a short time only," they might say. You might also hear "Act now and save." Companies use these ads to rush you through the buying process. They know that people who buy in a hurry often spend more money than they planned to.

Spotting the Tricks

Companies have been using advertising for many years. Most companies use advertising because they just want to make sure everyone knows about their products. Some companies are sneakier, though. They use these kinds of tricks. If you're not careful, it's easy to fall for them. An ad might get you to pay too much for a product. You might buy something you don't really want or need. You might not get what you pay for. You might be very unhappy.

The important rule about spending money is to think before you buy. Look at ads carefully before you decide to buy anything. Take time to think about what they're selling. Notice what the ads are using to get your attention. Try to decide why you want the product and if you really need it. Make sure to read the offer carefully. Look for any hidden costs or extra rules. Decide whether the product you want is worth the cost. Wait a few days before buying.

Taking these steps will help you become a smart shopper. Remember that the final decision about spending your money is always up to you. Pay attention and you'll spot the tricks.

4. Would the author say that you are a smart shopper? Explain why you are or are not.

Do the Right Thing—Wrap-Up

 Fill in the circle of the correct answer.

1. This passage is mostly about—
   Ⓐ how to save money when you are shopping for food.
   Ⓑ young people who have gotten into trouble shopping.
   Ⓒ why famous people make advertisements.
   Ⓓ how to be a careful shopper.

2. Which of the following tips did Claudia need when she joined the CD club?
   Ⓐ Before you sign up, make sure you know the details.
   Ⓑ If you buy a "free test," you might get stuck with a bill.
   Ⓒ Just because famous people say they like it, you might not.
   Ⓓ Don't buy in a hurry just because an ad says to buy now.

3. What does the author say is the most important rule about advertising?
   Ⓐ Use famous people to advertise.
   Ⓑ Get people to buy quickly.
   Ⓒ Tell the truth.
   Ⓓ Lie if you need to.

4. What advice does the author give to young people?
   Ⓐ There are always easy ways for you to save money.
   Ⓑ It can be fun to buy things you don't really need.
   Ⓒ Take your time and think before you buy.
   Ⓓ If other people say they like it, you will, too.

5. Name three ways that companies try to trick people into buying something. _____

   _____

6. Write a summary of the author's advice in this passage.

   _____

   _____

Answer Key

A Life in Their Hands

Page 9
1. The first answer is provided.
2. wrestler
3. stride
4. admit
5. escalator
6. paramedic
7. warning
8. renamed
9. challenge
10. rugged

Pages 10–14
For questions in this section, answers will vary.

Page 15
1. D
2. D
3. B
4. A
5. Answers will vary.
6. Answers will vary.

Page 16
Answers to the Idea Web in this section will vary.

Page 17
Answers will vary. Check that topic meets guidelines and supporting ideas are well developed.

Page 18
Students should circle the following words:
1. phone
2. rough
3. tough
4. laugh
5. Phoenix
6. enough
7. elephant
8. photograph

Page 19
1.–3. Accept all reasonable responses.

To Reach the Top

Page 20
For questions in this section, answers will vary.

Page 21
Across
1. The first answer is provided.
4. oxygen
5. sardines
6. triumph
7. altitude
8. increased

Down
1. zone
2. risk
3. expedition
5. summit

Pages 22–26
For questions in this section, answers will vary.

Page 27
1. B
2. A
3. D
4. A
5. Answers will vary.
6. Answers will vary.

Page 28
Answers to the Idea Chart in this section will vary.

Page 29
Answers will vary. Check that topic is clearly defined and ideas are well developed.

Page 30
Students should circle the following words:
1. were
2. adventure
3. together
4. first
5. Everest, higher, other
6. Climbers, danger, hurt
7. harder, dirt
8. safer, circle, sure

Page 31
1. dangerous
2. long   difficult
3. brave   careful
4. success

A Sudden Storm

Page 32
For questions in this section, answers will vary.

Page 33
1. The first answer is provided.
2. counselors
3. impressed
4. terrified
5. campsites
6. tightened
7. canoeists
8. skits
9. crafts
10. wilderness

Pages 34–38
For questions in this section, answers will vary.

Page 39
1. B
2. C
3. B
4. A
5. Answers will vary.
6. Answers will vary.

Page 40
Answers for the Planning Chart in this section will vary.

Page 41
Answers will vary. Check that letter fulfills the purpose and is convincing.

Page 42
Students should circle the following words:
1. short
2. perform
3. honor
4. scared
5. care
6. start
7. story
8. worm

Page 43
Answers will vary. Check that sentences use the correct meaning of each word.

Trash with Dash

Page 44
For questions in this section, answers will vary.

Page 45
Circled letters are noted with ().
1. societ(y)
2. t(o)ns
3. d(u)mpsters
4. dis(c)ard
5. inciner(a)tor
6. la(n)dfill
7. met(h)ane
8. acr(e)s
9. pol(l)utes
10. (p)oisonous
(You can help)

Pages 46–50
For questions in this section, answers will vary.

Page 51
1. D
2. A
3. A
4. C
5. Answers will vary.
6. Answers will vary.

Page 52
Answers for the Idea Chart will vary.

Page 53
Answers will vary. Check that the topic is clearly defined and supporting details are well developed.

Page 54
Students should circle the following words:
1. look
2. neighborhood

Students should underline the following words:
3. food
4. room

Circled words are notated by ().
Underlined words are underlined.
5. soon
6. (took) (look)
7. (good) school
8. (wood) too

Page 55
1. c. dangerous
2. a. to make smaller or less
3. b. to turn trash into something new
Answers will vary.
Answers will vary.
Answers will vary.

Count on Me—Wrap-Up

Pages 56–59
For questions in this section, answers will vary.

Page 60
1. B
2. A
3. B
4. A
5. Accept all reasonable responses.
6. Accept all reasonable responses.

Pages 61–64
For questions in this section, answers will vary.

Page 65
1. B
2. A
3. D
4. B
5. Accept all reasonable responses.

Saving the Zog

Page 68
For questions in this section, answers will vary.

Page 69
1. The first answer is provided.
2. respect
3. raiding
4. communicate
5. scarce
6. reaction
7. permission
8. hiccup
9. contact
10. authorities

Pages 70–74
For questions in this section, answers will vary.

Page 75
1. B
2. C
3. B
4. D
5. Answers will vary.
6. Answers will vary.

Page 76
Answers in the Idea Chart will vary.

Page 77
Answers will vary. Check that the topic of the speech fulfills the purpose and the reasons are convincing.

Page 78
Students should circle the following words:
1. down
2. allowed

Students should underline the following words:
3. know
4. grow

Circled words are notated by ().
Underlined words are underlined.
5. own, yellow
6. (how) knows
7. (frowns) (now)
8. show

Page 79
1. b. an animal that is kept or cared for
2. a. to pat
3. b. moved easily across
4. a. quickly or with shock
5. b. split or separated
6. b. at the starting place

The Fight for Right

Page 81
Across
2. The first answer is provided.
6. constitutional
8. fare
9. guilty
10. prison

Down
1. handcuffs
3. civil rights
4. minorities
5. fined
7. lawyer

Pages 82–86
For questions in this section, answers will vary.

Page 87
1. C
2. B
3. D
4. A
5. Answers will vary.
6. Answers will vary.

Page 88
Answers for the Idea Web in this section will vary.

Page 89
Answers will vary. Check that the essay is persuasive.

Reading Workout Book 2, SV 9781419099052

Page 90
1. thought, South
2. about
3. young
4. you, would
5. shout
6. could
7. group
8. your
9. double
10. bought

Page 91
1. raccoon and radar
2. three
3. 1
4. Answers will vary.

Ten-Book Summer
Page 93
1. The first answer is provided.
2. baby-sitter
3. teenager
4. cereal
5. amusement
6. bookcase
7. annoy
8. eased
9. assured
10. potential

Pages 94–98
For questions in this section, answers will vary.

Page 99
1. B
2. D
3. C
4. C
5. Answers will vary.
6. Answers will vary.

Page 100
Answers for the Idea Chart in this section will vary.

Page 101
Answers will vary. Check that the review is convincing and the opinion is clear.

Page 102
Students should circle the following words:
1. enjoy
2. disappointed
3. spoil
4. annoying
Students should write the following words on the lines.
5. boy
6. avoid
7. joy
8. choice

Page 103
1. nobody
2. teenaged
3. forever
4. girlfriend
5. anywhere
6. something

Tough Choices
Page 105
Circled letters are notated by ().
1. (p)rincipal
2. cultu(r)es
3. p(o)int of view
4. arg(u)ment
5. backgroun(d)s
6. opin(i)on
7. a(d)vice
8. (e)laboration
9. deb(a)te
10. per(s)uasive
Answer: She is **proud** to teach **ideas**.

Page 106–110
For questions in this section, answers will vary.

Page 111
1. C
2. A
3. B
4. A
5. Answers will vary.
6. Answers will vary.

Page 112
Answers for the Graphic Organizer in this section will vary.

Page 113
Answers will vary. Check that the topic is clearly defined and supporting details are well developed.

Page 114
Students should circle the following words:
1. thoughts
2. writing
3. high
4. knowledge
Circled letters are notated by ().
5. ri(gh)t
6. (k)now
7. (w)rong
8. fi(gh)t

Page 115
1. rewrite
2. review
3. recycle
4. returned

Do the Right Thing—Wrap-Up
Pages 116–119
For questions in this section, answers will vary.

Page 120
1. C
2. A
3. C
4. A
5. A
6. Answers will vary.

Pages 121–124
For questions in this section, answers will vary.

Page 125
1. D
2. A
3. C
4. C
5. Answers will vary.
6. Answers will vary.

Answer Key
Reading Workout Book 2, SV 9781419099052